Northern Sandscapes

Northern Sandscapes

Exploring Saskatchewan's Athabasca Sand Dunes

Robin and Arlene Karpan

PARKLAND
PUBLISHING

Saskatoon

Text, illustrations and photographs Copyright © 1998 by Robin and Arlene Karpan.

All rights reserved. No part of this book may be reproduced or used in any form by any means—graphic, electronic, mechanical, including photocopying, recording, taping, or any information storage and retrieval system—without permission in writing from the publisher, except by a reviewer who may quote brief passages of text in a review.

Designed by Robin and Arlene Karpan.

Published in Canada in 1998 by

Parkland Publishing
501 Mount Allison Place
Saskatoon, Saskatchewan
Canada S7H 4A9
(306) 242-7731
e-mail: parkland@skyport.com
web site: www.skyport.com/parkland/books

Printed in Canada by

Houghton Boston
709 – 43rd Street East
Saskatoon, Saskatchewan S7K 0V7
(306) 664-3458

Color scanning and film output by Houghton Boston. Printed on acid free paper.

Canadian Cataloguing in Publication Data

Karpan, Robin.
    Northern sandscapes

    Includes bibliographical references and index.
    ISBN 0-9683579-0-3

1. Athabasca Sand Dunes (Sask. and Alta.) – Description and travel. 2. Sand dunes – Athabasca, Lake, Region (Sask. and Alta.) – Description and travel. I. Karpan, Arlene. II. Title.

FC3545.A83 K37 1998   917.124′1   C98-920068-X
F1074.A83 K37 1998

While every effort has been made to ensure that the information contained in this publication is correct, the authors and publisher accept no responsibility or liability for errors, omissions, loss, injury or inconvenience sustained as a result of information contained in this publication. The authors and publisher caution against using this publication as the sole source of information for visiting the Athabasca Sand Dunes or other wilderness areas, and advise contacting provincial park authorities for complete and current information on visiting these areas. Errors brought to the attention of the publisher will be corrected in subsequent editions.

PREVIOUS PAGE: *The sand-clogged William River close to its delta. The "rows" of light and dark vegetation in the upper part of the frame are ancient beach ridges, separated by low areas of mostly peat bog.*

Acknowledgements

Numerous people provided advice, assistance, and encouragement throughout this project. Dr. Vernon Harms, Curator of the W.P. Fraser Herbarium at the University of Saskatchewan, provided helpful information and suggestions on rare plants, as did as Dr. Ellen Macdonald and Dr. Brett Purdy of the University of Alberta, and Brent Zettl of Prairie Plant Systems in Saskatoon. Jeff Whiting of Resource Intelligence Service Consulting provided numerous helpful comments on geology, hydrology, and other technical matters. Dr. Walter Kupsch of the Geological Sciences Department of the University of Saskatchewan provided comments on some of the geological formations. Dr. Hartmut Usinger and Dr. Christoph Lange of the University of Kiel in Germany provided comments on Athabasca's ventifacts. Tim Jones, Executive Director of the Saskatchewan Archaeological Society, provided comments on Athabasca's prehistory. Frank Roy, Alan Smith of the Canadian Wildlife Service, Tim Trottier and Dave Phillips of Saskatchewan Environment and Resource Management (SERM), were very helpful in updating the check-list of birds. We especially appreciate the assistance of those who read over the entire manuscript and provided numerous useful suggestions, including Frank Roy, Peter Kingsmill, Jeff Whiting and various people in Saskatchewan Environment and Resource Management.

Valuable advice and suggestions were offered by SERM officials including park manager Kevin Weatherbee in La Ronge, and George Bihun in Stony Rapids. We especially acknowledge the assistance and encouragement of Ken Lozinsky, Manager of Park Management Services, Parks and Facilities Branch, who shared our belief that public awareness and education can play an important role in protecting fragile environments such as the Athabasca Sand Dunes.

The interpretation of comments provided to us by these and other people are entirely our own, and any errors that may have crept into this book are also entirely our own.

Sponsors of the Project

This book would not have been possible without the support of our sponsors and their confidence in our project. Randy Williams and the staff of Tourism Saskatchewan have been especially helpful not only in providing assistance for this project, but also in recognizing the importance of Saskatchewan's natural environment and encouraging responsible ecotourism.

We have received tremendous support from Cliff and Stella Blackmur of Athabasca Eco Expeditions and their entire staff at Otherside River Lodge. Besides arranging the logistics for our trips and making the aerial photography possible, Cliff was responsible for introducing us to many scenic wonders of Saskatchewan's far north and getting us hooked on this very special land.

Contents

Introduction   11

William River   15
    Canoeing to the Dunes   15
    Braids of Gold   23
    In a Desert Garden   30
    Desert-like but not a Desert   37
    In the Shadow of Giants   41
    Butterscotch Pudding and Whipped Cream   47
    Up the Creek   48

Lake Athabasca   55
    Thomson Bay   55
    Enchanted Forests   58
    Stories in the Sand   68
    Stories from the Past   71
    The Fur Trade   73
    Boom and Bust   75
    Pink Clouds and Warm Breezes   79
    Archibald River   81
    Stranded   88

MacFarlane River   95
    Land of the Giant Beaver   96
    Waterfalls and Pickup Sticks   103

Photographing the Dunes   105

Visiting the Athabasca Sand Dunes   111

Appendix I   Check-list of Rare Plants of
    Saskatchewan's Athabasca Sand Dunes   118
Appendix II   Check-list of Birds:
    Athabasca Sand Dunes Area   120
Appendix III   Check-list of Mammals:
    Athabasca Sand Dunes Area   123

Bibliography   124

Index   126

About the Authors   128

The William River just downstream from where its powerful rapids change to a meandering, braided stream clogged with sand.

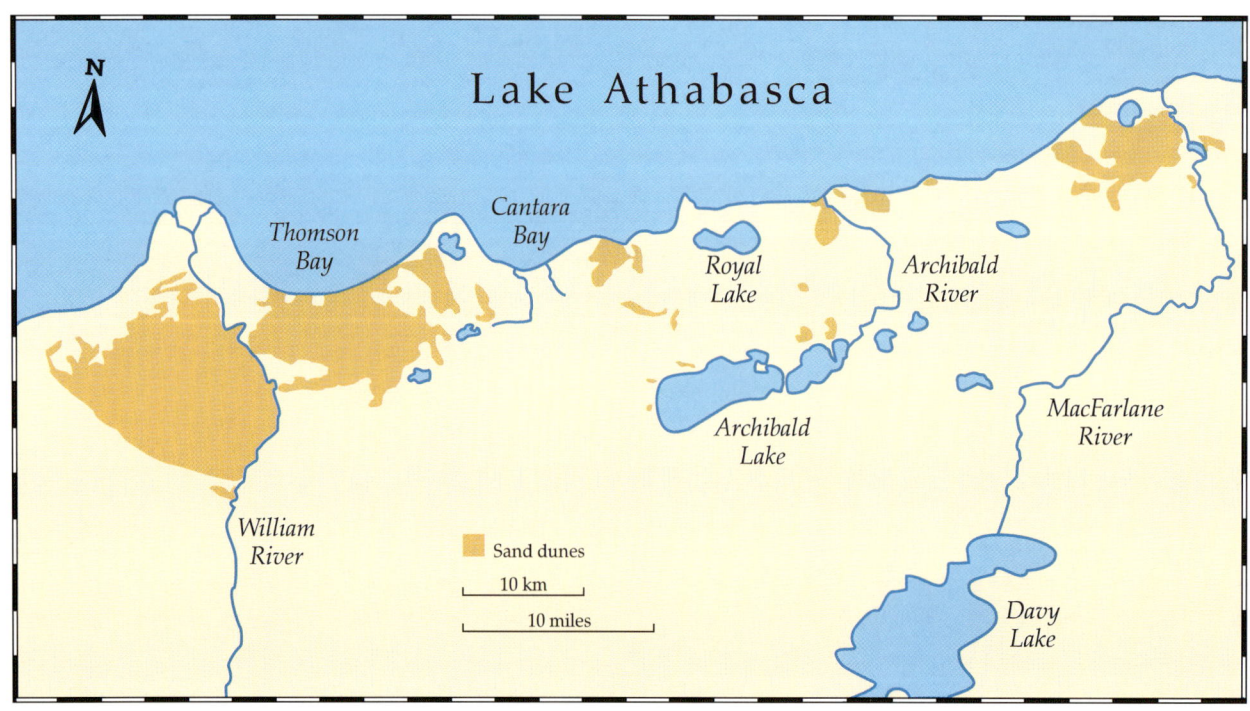

Introduction

A long time ago a giant went hunting beavers along Lake Athabasca. The beavers had built a dam across the great lake, so the giant broke it open to lower the water and find the beavers. Spotting a beaver, the giant threw a spear at it, and thinking he had killed it, tossed it on the south shore of the lake. But the beaver wasn't dead and it kicked up the soil to such an extent that it was ground into sand. And that, according to a local Dene legend, is how the Athabasca Sand Dunes came to be.

Scientists have a more complex explanation involving retreating glaciers and sandstone sediments. But when we saw this strange and wild landscape for the first time, it wasn't at all difficult to relate to stories of mythical giants.

The Athabasca Sand Dunes are like nowhere else on Earth—the largest active dune fields in Canada, among the most northerly major dunes in the world, a desert-like environment seemingly misplaced in the midst of the northern forest. Athabasca Sand Dunes Provincial Wilderness Park preserves a series of dune fields, as well as rivers, lakes and forest, stretching for about 100 kilometres along the south shore of Lake Athabasca.

It's a special place where we can land our canoe on an exquisite beach in mid-summer and not find a single human footprint. Instead we find flowering plants that grow only here, tree roots two metres above ground, springs emerging from sand, towering dunes with sinuous knife-edge crests, and ghostly skeletons of ancient forests turning blood red with the glow of twilight. We paddle down the William River with a sense of wonder at how it weaves through forest and sand. Then when we fly over, the river becomes a beautiful abstract painting that only Mother Nature could create. If we had to choose one word to describe the Athabasca Sand Dunes, it would surely be "magical".

Our love affair with the dunes began in 1990 with a canoe trip down the William River

and along the south shore of Lake Athabasca while on assignment for *Canadian Geographic* magazine. We were immediately hooked, and returned every chance we had. We are fortunate to have visited and photographed spectacular landscapes in many parts of the world, but this was different, not only visually but spiritually, profoundly affecting how we felt about the wilderness. It was not an exotic landscape in some far-flung corner of the globe. It was an exotic landscape right in our own back yard, a unique part of our natural heritage.

We hope that our book will help foster an appreciation of this special place, and that those who travel there will be aware of its fragile nature and the need to tread lightly. Whether or not we visit remote wilderness landscapes such as the Athabasca Sand Dunes, it is reassuring that such places still exist, where nature's mysteries haven't all been solved and where the magic continues.

The William River's complex riverbed as seen from an airplane. Most of the sand visible here is under water; the dark hues are deep channels while the light hues indicate sand covered by only a few centimetres of water. Sand bars above the water appear bright white, such as the one in the lower left part of the picture.

William River

The contrast between the two banks of the William River was striking. It was as if we were paddling along a narrow ribbon between two worlds. To the east stretched the familiar jack pine and birch forest of northern Saskatchewan. But to the west we could see only massive banks of golden sand rising up to 30 metres straight out of the water.

Canoeing to the Dunes

While the idea seemed strange at first, we decided that the best way to explore Canada's largest sand dunes would be by canoe. It would give us access to all the major dune fields along Lake Athabasca's south shore. But more important, we could follow the entire eastern edge of the great William River dune field, the largest and most spectacular part of the Athabasca Sand Dunes.

The area south of Lake Athabasca is part of the Athabasca Plain Ecoregion, a Precambrian sandstone formation which sits on top of the Precambrian Shield. Covering about 100,000 square kilometres, the Athabasca sandstone formation extends south to Cree Lake, east to Wollaston Lake and west to just across the Alberta border.

About 13,000–14,000 years ago, the great Keewatin ice field started receding, forming large glacial lakes. As these lakes drained, the sandy plain south of Lake Athabasca was exposed around 9,000 years ago. Meltwater from the retreating glaciers flowed through the William and MacFarlane spillways, depositing sandstone sediment in the form of deltas in Glacial Lake Athabasca. These sediments were exposed as the glacial lake receded and the land rebounded after the weight of the glacial ice was gone. Strong winds eventually formed the sandy sediments into dunes. It is believed that until 4,000–5,000 years ago, there were no forests here to slow the effects of the wind.

LEFT: *A birch tree along the William River is undermined as the wind blows away the sandy ground and exposes the tree's roots.*

Carswell Lake.

For thousands of years the active dunes were sustained by new sources of sand exposed in the river deltas and beaches. Wind and wave action redistributed sand along the south shore. Forest fires also played a role, periodically destroying vegetation which managed to take hold and allowing the wind to form sandy blowouts which grew into dunes. Most dune fields are on the Saskatchewan side of the lake, although two are also found in Alberta.

Our journey began at the south end of Carswell Lake, about 80 kilometres south of Lake Athabasca. It was a pleasant paddle to the north end of the long narrow lake, past rocky cliffs, pebble-covered shores and inviting sandy beaches. After setting up camp we went fishing for our supper. The first cast brought a northern pike so big that it easily slithered out of the small flimsy net we had brought along to save space and weight. A few more casts and we hauled in an even larger monster, which we released because it was much too big for two people to eat. The fish after that tore right through the net, leaving a gaping hole in the webbing. Almost ready to give up and opt for a dried food concoction instead, we caught a pike that was just the right size.

Not at all our typical fishing experience. Usually we struggle to catch something big enough to eat—not small enough. Perhaps this was an omen of what the trip ahead would bring. But was it a sign of grandeur and plenty, or a sign that we were tackling more than we could handle?

Massive sand dunes tower over a stretch of rapids and rock gardens on the William River.

The next morning we made a short portage to the Carswell River and were just beginning to enjoy being helped along by the current when we hit a set of shallow rapids, the first of dozens we had to contend with over the next few days. Long stretches of the river were littered with rock gardens, with boulders of all sizes protruding above the water or hiding just under the surface.

In many places we walked the canoe through, trying to find water deep enough to keep the canoe afloat while guiding it through each rocky maze. Often moving at a snail's pace so as not to twist an ankle between the slippery boulders, we took up to three hours along some stretches—wading, dragging and scraping over rocks that left their marks in countless gouges on the bottom of the canoe. At one point we became hopelessly stuck and had no choice but to unload in mid-river then haul the canoe and all the gear downstream to deeper water. We were beginning to wonder if we were canoeing to Lake Athabasca or walking. Fortunately, the late June weather varied between warm and hot and the water felt refreshingly cool.

It wasn't necessary to portage until we came to a powerful set of rapids where the

The last stretch of rapids on the William River.

Carswell narrows as it empties into the much larger William River. Although the William was wider, deeper and swifter, we still faced long stretches of rapids and rock gardens. We ran some sections, portaged around a few rough places and waded through others, always erring on the side of caution. We were alone and our emergency radio was either out of range or not working properly. We couldn't afford mistakes.

For most of our journey down the William, we saw little evidence of people. In a couple spots, remains of rusted square-shaped tin cans poked through the vegetation on the forest floor, looking like they belonged to another era. Between Carswell Lake and Lake Athabasca, we saw no recent garbage at all—not a single beer can, gum wrapper or plastic bag.

Our map showed that we were approaching the southernmost extent of the William River dunes, but when we rounded a curve and saw a huge bank of sand rising from the river's edge, it still took us by surprise. What struck us most was the abrupt change, the dark green forested bank suddenly giving way to a wall of gold. Impressive as it was, we hadn't yet arrived at the main dune field, but rather at a large "orphaned" sand dune just to the south. As we paddled north, forest replaced sand on the west bank for about four kilometres. Then the sand appeared again and stretched as far west and north as we could see; we had reached the main William River dune field.

For the next 25 kilometres or so, the William's west bank varied from gently rising

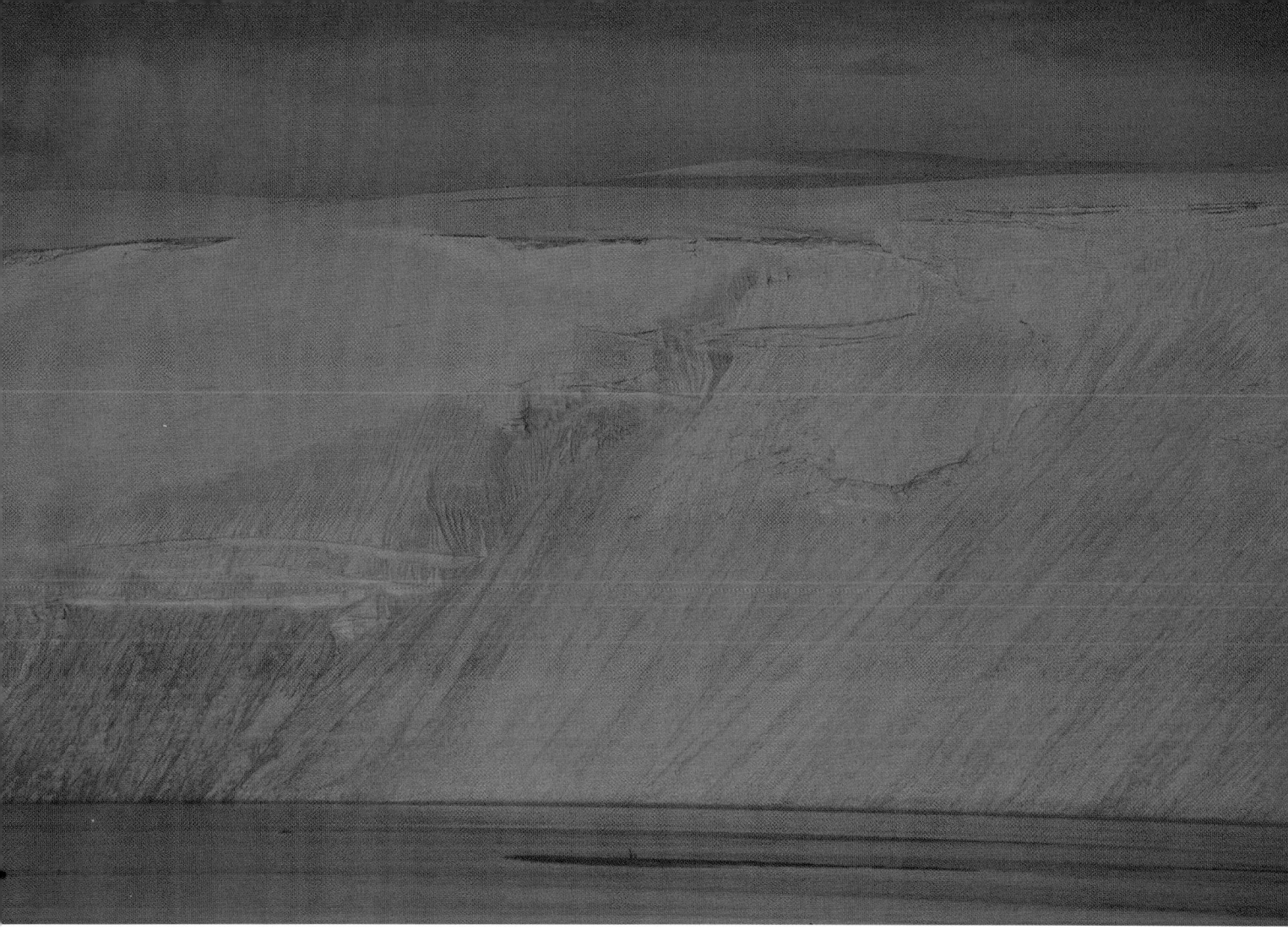

The sandy west bank of the William River glows just before sunrise.

sand hills to 30-metre high precipitous sand faces dropping into the water. The bank was also dotted with splashes of green as clumps of vegetation, including stands of tall trees, clung to life despite the constant advance of sand. The dune field stretches west as far as 15 kilometres and covers 166 square kilometres. Prevailing winds keep moving massive amounts of sand eastward to the river, but amazingly little crosses the water to the forested east bank. The William's swift current takes all the sand it is given, carrying some 3,000 tonnes per day to Lake Athabasca.

It was along this stretch that we encountered the most whitewater and rock gardens. Some rapids were like mini waterfalls as the river plunged over rocky shelves. It was slow going but we were treated to some of the most spectacular scenery of the trip. Since there are no marked portages along this little-travelled river, we walked the crests of the enormous dunes overlooking the river to scout the best routes through or around the rapids.

Where we had to portage, we could either struggle through the forest on the east bank or head over the dunes on the west bank. Portaging a canoe over sand dunes had two

OVERLEAF: *Camping on a sand bar which extends from the William River's east bank. The west bank of the river along this stretch consists of pure sand slip faces.*

ABOVE: *Looking over the William River.* TOP LEFT: *Sand patterns above and below the surface of the water in the William River.* BOTTOM LEFT: *Three different depths of sand converge in the William River. The darkest area is about one metre below the surface, the brown sand on the bottom is about 20 centimetres below the surface, and the light sand on top is just below the water surface.*

advantages—no trees to run into and fewer mosquitoes. But the advantages ended there. When we walked on the level, the fine sand felt reasonably stable, but climbing even a slight incline with a load meant sinking ankle deep with every step. Then there was the ever-present wind. Carrying a canoe over the open dunes was like trying to carry a hang glider.

Braids of Gold

In this land of surprises, the seemingly unending rapids suddenly ended, as if a line were drawn and we had left one river and entered another dramatically different one. About 17 kilometres before emptying into Lake Athabasca, the William spread into a wide, sand-choked braided stream with no rocks or even small stones anywhere in sight. The transformation was astonishing, from the roar of a mighty river to the gentle trickle of a meandering stream.

William River.

Just beyond the end of the rapids, the wide river became clogged with sand bars and small islands. Here sand enters the William not only from the west bank but also from the east bank where a narrow tongue of the Thomson Bay dune field extends all the way from Lake Athabasca to the river.

We climbed to the top of the dunes on the west bank. Below us the smooth slip faces dropped into the water 30 metres below, while the east bank was covered in patches of green and gold as trees and sand struggled for dominance. A maze of sand bars cluttered the river, while below the surface of the water sand of different depths and hues formed beautiful abstract patterns.

Not all of the sand bars are visible above the water surface. Scientists estimate that underwater sand bars covering the riverbed move downstream at the rate of about 10 metres per day. The pattern of sand movement has been compared to that of the tracks of a bulldozer. Grains of sand are carried over the top of the bar, then slide down the downstream face of the bar, becoming temporarily suspended. When the river erodes the back of the bar, newly exposed grains of sand are transported up and forward. We could watch the suspended sand moving and every so often we saw large "turbulence" bubbles come to the surface, as air pockets were formed by water flowing over the complex river bottom.

At first glance it looked as if there was plenty of water in the river, but as we were to discover, most of it was extremely shallow. Eroded channels well over a metre deep cut

Trying to find deep water in the William River.

through the sandy river bottom, often along the river's edge where dense stands of willows prevent the bank from eroding and allow the channel to form. But even the forested east bank gets so clogged with sand in places that the channels simply end and start up somewhere else.

It was a challenge keeping the canoe in the deeper channels which often zigzagged from one side of the river to the other. We constantly watched the color of the water change just ahead of us—chocolate brown meant deep water, golden brown meant shallow but probably passable, and light amber meant that we would soon be walking. Often the channels ended so abruptly that we were left grounded on a sand bank just below the water surface. We would then have to get out and guide, and occasionally drag, the canoe to the nearest deep water.

Travelling downstream wasn't too difficult, as the current helped us skim across some shallow sections. Paddling upstream, as we did on later trips, was an entirely different story. It was enough of an effort going against the current in deep water, but in the shallow sections we found it difficult to get much power when our paddles barely got wet before sticking in the sand.

Getting out of the canoe in mid-stream was sometimes a surprise. In most places the river bottom felt reasonably stable, considering

ABOVE: *Sand bar in the William River.* TOP RIGHT: *The Thomson Bay dune field looms above the trees along the William River's east bank.* BELOW RIGHT: *West bank of the William River.*

that the sand is moving almost constantly. But once in a while we would step out of the canoe and immediately start sinking in quicksand fashion. This usually happened close to sand bars near shore where the pressure of groundwater helps keep the sand from settling. But that sinking feeling was more of a nuisance than a danger; we usually didn't have to go far to find more solid footing or deeper water to float the canoe.

Once we found a deep channel the William's current would carry us at a fair speed. Along one channel near the east bank, a black bear emerged from the thick bushes just in front of us and began swimming across the river without bothering to check for traffic. We were headed straight for it. What to do? If we tried to veer off or stop we would likely end up grounded on a sand bar close to a surprised bear. On the other hand, running into a bear with a canoe didn't seem very smart either. Just before we were forced to make a quick decision, the bear glanced our way, then gave us a startled look. Its head went down, its feet shot up and with a thunderous splash it did a complete flip, quickly swam back to shore and escaped, thrashing through the willows as we glided past, quite relieved.

Bears are among the most common large animals, and the most unpredictable. We set

up camp on a sand bar which extends from the east bank of the William River and overlooks some of the highest pure sand slip faces on the west bank. It would be difficult to imagine a more gorgeous spot. We noticed a few bear tracks in the area when we arrived, but they appeared old and didn't cause us undue concern. Besides, it was difficult to find places to camp that didn't have bear tracks.

We were half way through eating a late supper when an enormous black bear ambled out of the thick bush and headed directly toward our camp. He struck us as the type that walked wherever he pleased. Obviously the tracks we had seen earlier weren't his. We made as much noise as possible and the bear finally stopped, rose up to sniff the air, then casually turned and slowly disappeared into the bush. We got the impression that he wasn't going far. It seemed prudent to break camp and find another spot a bit farther down river. We could always return in the morning to complete our photography and, after all, this was the bear's territory, not ours.

Looking northwest towards Lake Athabasca. The William River is lined mostly by sand on its west bank (upper left) and forest along its east bank. The sand at the bottom of the picture is part of the Thomson Bay dune field which stretches northeast to Lake Athabasca.

Sand chickweed (Stellaria arenicola) *growing in the dune field west of the William River. This plant is endemic to the Athabasca Sand Dunes.*

In a Desert Garden

When Athabasca Sand Dunes was declared a provincial wilderness park in 1992, it was because of its unique plant life as much as its spectacular scenery. The vegetation varies throughout the park. Semi-open stands of jack pine with a ground cover of lichen and scattered blueberry are most common on the uplands and dry forest areas, while mature stands of white spruce dominate the south shore of Lake Athabasca. Tall stands of black spruce are common on some moist river banks and deltas, and stunted black spruce, tamarack, Labrador tea and leatherleaf often line the open bogs and small lakes. But it's the vegetation of the active dunes that makes the Athabasca Sand Dunes botanically unique. Indeed, botanists consider this one of the most important centres of rare and endemic plants in Canada.

Of the more than 300 plants that grow here, 52 are considered rare in Saskatchewan. Two of these, bog adder's-mouth (*Malaxis paludosa*) and narrow-leaved sundew (*Drosera linearis*), are also considered rare in Canada. Ten plants—five broad leaved herbs, four willows and one grass—are endemic, meaning that they are native to and restricted to the south shore of Lake Athabasca and are found

*Mother Nature's garden near the William River—fireweed (back), the endemic felt-leaved willow (*Salix silicicola*) on the right, and the endemic floccose tansy (*Tanacetum huronense* var. *floccosum*) in front.*

nowhere else on Earth. (See Appendix I for a check-list of rare and endemic plants.)

The endemic plants are derived from Arctic, boreal forest and great plains plants that moved into the area after the retreat of the glaciers and warming of the climate. The sand dunes acted as a habitat island in the middle of the boreal forest where some plants became isolated and had to adapt to new conditions. They developed distinctly from their parent populations and evolved into new plants.

This evolution was not the same for all plants, stressed Dr. Brett Purdy of the Sustainable Forest Management Network at the University of Alberta. In his report to the World Wildlife Fund on genetic variation in Athabasca's endemic plants, Dr. Purdy indicated that each endemic revealed its own secrets and had its own unique history, but that there is still much more to be discovered. What is unique here is the high number of endemics, more comparable to the southern part of North America than to the north. Few endemic plants occur in the boreal forest and Arctic regions of North America, and indeed the world, leaving scientists with an intriguing evolutionary puzzle: why did they develop here?

It's tough to be a plant in the Athabasca Sand Dunes. To survive, a plant has to get by on little moisture, withstand abrasion from blowing sand, and burial by moving dunes. Sand chickweed (*Stellaria arenicola*), an endemic with tiny white flowers, often grows in

Endemic plants.
ABOVE, AND OPPOSITE PAGE: *Felt-leaved willow* (Salix silicicola).
BELOW RIGHT: *Sand-loving barrenground willow* (Salix brachycarpa *var.* psammophila).
LEFT, AND BELOW LEFT: *Inland sea-thrift* (Armeria maritima *ssp.* interior).

clumps in active sand. Despite its delicate look, this hardy plant has phenomenal staying power. University of Alberta forest ecologist, Dr. Ellen Macdonald, found that one of her study plots of sand chickweed had been completely covered by sand during a wind storm. The plants soon emerged, however, and by the end of the season were the same height as plants that had escaped burial.

The inland sea-thrift (*Armeria maritima* ssp. *interior*) is perhaps the most exotic looking endemic. Its ball-shaped head, about two centimetres across, is covered in minute reddish-purple flowers. Each head sits on a thin stalk about 20 centimetres long, looking like a tiny candy apple stuck in the sand. One of the rarer plants, inland sea-thrift grows in various parts of the dunes, including areas mostly devoid of other vegetation.

Impoverished pinweed (*Lechea intermedia* var. *depauperata*) is the most difficult endemic to find. In fact, it has only been found in four locations. It grows in small dense carpets in sandy soils where jack pine woods are regrowing after a fire, and in partially wet areas such as the flats of receding shores. Transient in nature, it temporarily colonizes very specific habitats then disappears.

Dr. Vernon Harms, curator of the W.P. Fraser Herbarium at the University of Saskatchewan and one of the leading authorities on Athabasca's plants, calls impoverished pinweed a plant "surviving on the edge". He stresses that forest fire suppression could be detrimental to this plant since it seems to need forest fires to survive. The establishment of a provincial wilderness park is generally seen as very positive for the protection of rare plants.

ABOVE: *The endemic Tyrrell's willow* (Salix planifolia *ssp.* tyrrellii). ABOVE LEFT: *Sea lyme-grass* (Elymus mollis) *and felt-leaved willow on a sand dune overlooking the William River.* BELOW LEFT: *The endemic floccose tansy* (Tanacetum huronense *var.* floccosum).

It is especially fortunate for the impoverished pinweed, since wilderness park policy is that forest fires should not be suppressed, as fires are part of nature.

Two of Athabasca's endemics, inland sea-thrift and Tyrrell's willow (*Salix tyrrellii*), are considered Threatened in Canada by COSEWIC (Committee on the Status of Endangered Wildlife in Canada). Impoverished pinweed has been recommended for the same designation. Dr. Harms cautions against reading too much into the listing, pointing out that other endemics and national rarities of the area may be just as deserving of a COSEWIC designation. One reason these plants are officially recognized is that they have been subject to COSEWIC status reports. Not all of the plants have been studied to the same extent.

One of the most abundant endemics is the aptly named felt-leaved willow (*Salix silicicola*), with large silvery-green leaves that have a fuzzy velvet or felt-like texture. They were part of the scenery almost everywhere we went in the dunes, from sand banks overlooking the William River to Lake Athabasca's south shore and even part way into the dune fields. Although they are found nowhere else on Earth, here they are downright common.

Sea lyme-grass (*Elymus mollis*) is also very common, usually growing in mounded sandy clumps. Considered rare in Saskatchewan, it's normally found in Arctic maritime areas of Canada. No one is sure how it got here. The Vikings reportedly used sea lyme-grass as a food source, leading to some imaginative conjecture as to where the Vikings may have ended up. Early fur traders from Hudson Bay also used it as padding in their boots. It is believed, however, that sea lyme-grass has been here for a long time and is a native rather than

Common pink wintergreen.

an introduced plant.

The largest number of plants in the dunes are found in the dune slacks, the mostly flat troughs between sand ridges where the water table is close to the ground surface. These areas act like nurseries, providing habitat to get some plants started before they invade the drier active sand dunes. Dune slacks close to the William River resemble exotic desert gardens, where a variety of endemics as well as common plants thrive completely surrounded by shifting sand.

The rare plants of Athabasca may be a useful source of genetic material for reclaiming land disturbed by mining. Uranium mining takes place in the southern part of the Athabasca Plain. The jack pine forest is removed for a mine site, leaving sandy soil. Brent Zettl, president of Prairie Plant Systems in Saskatoon, works with mining companies on reclamation projects. His research showed it was more effective to first plant primary native species such as dune grasses rather than to begin with jack pine or other species which require more soil and stabilized conditions. Once the primary plants stabilize the soil, other vegetation will grow.

As they can survive in unstable sandy soil, primary native plants growing in the Athabasca Sand Dunes were found to have the most potential. The provincial park allowed the collection of a small amount of seeds which were planted in trial plots. The plan is to grow enough seed for reclamation so that it won't be necessary to return to the dunes for more material.

Sand heather.

Other research is taking place using dune plants to reclaim sandy soils disturbed by heavy oil extraction in the Athabasca tar sands of northern Alberta. While still in the early stages, pilot tests looked promising.

For anyone who enjoys the beauty of nature, the appeal of Athabasca's plant life goes well beyond what is rare or exotic. We found pleasant surprises everywhere we went. The sundew is a bright red insect-eating plant with tiny tentacle-like hairs, normally found in ponds. We saw several adding color to the dune slacks and to sandy islands in the William River. Common pink wintergreen usually grows in moist woodlands, but we discovered a profuse patch on the edge of a small bush, totally surrounded by sand dunes. Sand heather in bloom covered the sand with a delicate yellow carpet, while flowering fireweed and wild roses added splashes of magenta and deep pink. Here, even the commonplace became special.

Desert-like but not a Desert

Just west of the William River are vast areas of desert pavement, a thin carpet of stones and pebbles on top of the sand. Found in all of Athabasca's major dune fields, the formation is also referred to as gravel pavement, or as "gobi" after the Gobi Desert in China

ABOVE: *Desert pavement in the William River dune field.* RIGHT: *Many stones on the desert pavement have been eroded into different shapes by constant sandblasting.*

where it is common.

The stones are not packed together, as in gravel, but spaced apart so that they seldom touch each other. The "pavement" is formed by a process called deflation where strong winds winnow away grains of sand, leaving stones ranging in size from pea-sized pebbles to larger cobbles and even boulders. Although the formation is usually only one stone deep, it protects the sand underneath from further erosion. In some places the stones were pushed in by ice and deposited during the era of the glacial lakes, some 9,000 years ago. In other places, level expanses of desert pavement coincide with the former bottom of the glacial lake.

The stones often have a shiny appearance from being continuously sandblasted and polished. Most intriguing are the ventifacts, Latin for "made by the wind"; stones that have been eroded into different shapes. Some ventifacts have a flat or slightly concave sandblasted side or facet. Others have two sandblasted sides, joined by a sharp ridge or keel. Ventifacts with one keel are called "Einkanter"; those with three sandblasted sides and three keels, often forming a pyramid shape, are known as "Dreikanter". Many Athabasca ventifacts have three sides but are shaped like Brazil nuts rather than pyramids.

Sandblasting on more than one side can occur if the stone moves, such as when the sand it rests on is undermined, or when the direction of the wind changes. The longest

keel in most Athabasca ventifacts has a northeast to southwest orientation, with one of the sandblasted sides facing the prevailing northwest winds. This is what we might expect. But many ventifacts are sandblasted and polished on the southeast side as well. Scientists indicate that in the distant past, perhaps several thousand years ago, Athabasca's prevailing winds came from a different direction than they do today.

While ventifacts are found in many parts of the world, Athabasca's are considered quite special. Two ventifact experts from the University of Kiel in Germany, who recently visited major ventifact sites throughout North America, called Athabasca the highlight. Dr.

The slip face, or precipitation ridge, of a sand dune buries the forest as the dune migrates east.

Christoph Lange indicated that the sandstone ventifacts here were some of the most abundant and beautiful he has ever seen. He referred to the ventifacts as very "sociable"; where he found some prime specimens, he usually found others nearby.

Desert pavement is among the most fragile landforms in the dunes; even footsteps remain visible for years. It is important to walk on the active sand surfaces that border the desert pavement, not on the pavement itself. It is likewise important to leave ventifacts undisturbed so that they continue to be a source of wonder.

As we hiked across the vast William River dune field with little in sight besides sand and more sand, it was difficult to believe that this isn't really a desert. Geologists categorize sand dunes in two broad groups—dry-sand dunes (or desert dunes) and moist-sand dunes (or parabolic dunes). The Athabasca Sand Dunes, and indeed all sand dunes in Canada, are part of the latter group. Periodically recharged by rain and snow, the sands of Athabasca have a moisture content of four to six percent.

Desert dunes are so dry that they freely respond to changes in wind speed and direction, while parabolic dunes have more cohesion and to some extent can resist movement by the wind. Studies indicate that moving sand with a moisture content of four percent requires double the wind velocity of that required to move dry sand.

The active dunes of Athabasca have a variety of styles. Some have a classic parabolic shape which is a crescent or U-shape with the

The dune field encroaches upon the forest as it migrates east.

convex side facing downwind and with trailing ridges, or wings, facing upwind. The wind scoops sand from the centre of the dune and blows it to the steeper convex side called the slip face or precipitation ridge. The sand is eventually forced over the ridge, causing the dune to move forward. The wings trail behind because of the drag caused by the moisture in the sand and by vegetation which tries to take hold.

Some of the dunes are transverse, with a long dune ridge perpendicular to the wind direction. Others are V-shaped, J-shaped or composites that incorporate different forms. Most of the sand sheet west of the William River has been referred to as rolling dunes, a gently rolling landscape with few steep slip faces. However, in the centre of the field lie 40 or so "giant dunes", the most dramatic of them all.

In the Shadow of Giants

The giant dunes weren't visible from the river; we could see only an endless expanse of sand broken by stretches of desert pavement. Hiking west of the river was disconcerting at first, much like walking into the centre of a desert. Isolated stands of willow, sea lymegrass and other patches of vegetation were scattered here and there, and these became

ABOVE AND LEFT: *The knife-edge crest of a giant dune.*

increasingly scarce as we continued farther west.

The animal and bird tracks that were common on the sand bordering the river all but disappeared. Only the tracks of a lone wolf continued for about 500 metres away from the river, but these too ended as the animal turned around and headed back to more familiar surroundings. The only sign of birdlife was a flock of about 20 Arctic terns, silently circling high above and obviously following us. Terns nest far into the dunes, often favoring desert pavement. As their nests were likely hidden nearby, they were keeping a close eye on our route.

After 45 minutes of walking over surprisingly solid sand, and gradually gaining altitude, we could see the long undulating shapes of the giant dunes shimmering in the distance. Someone once likened them to gigantic humpback whales in a sea of sand. Even though the dunes looked close, it took us another hour to reach them. It was impossible to follow a direct route as we had to walk around large areas of fragile desert pavement.

These impressive dunes, oriented northwest to southeast, rise as high as 35 metres, with some stretching over a kilometre in length. For the most part the dunes are free standing, a series of individual monsters rising from a level plain. The smaller dunes are rounded, but the tops of the larger ones have sharp knife-edge crests flowing in sinuous curves.

Strong winds from both the east and west help shape the sharp crests, and it is believed

Looking south from the top of a giant dune. These dunes are subject to opposing winds. Here, wind from the east helps shape the crest.

that these opposing winds are also responsible for keeping these dunes from migrating as much as the other Athabasca dunes. Much remains a mystery, however. No other part of the Athabasca Sand Dunes has aroused as much controversy among scientists as explaining and classifying these giant dunes. They have been called longitudinal dunes and seif dunes because of their long continuous ridges, transverse dunes because the wind hits the ridges at right angles, and oblique sand ridges because of the strong influence of opposing winds. Most of these dunes have a shallow crescent shape, convex to the east, leading to the interpretation that they are a type of parabolic dune. That these giants defy easy explanation makes them all the more intriguing.

It was an awesome sight as we stood at the eastern base of one of the monstrous dunes and looked up. Scattered bits of vegetation clung to the lower part, but above it was pure smooth sand, bellying out slightly before reaching the sharp crest some 30 metres above us.

Climbing to the top, we were amazed at the sharpness of the peak, with its precipitous drop to the east. The western side was just as steep near the top but farther down it became a more smooth, gradual slope. The wind had almost died at the base of the dune, but up here it was still howling away, filling the air with fine grains while continuing to sculpt the crest.

The wind can be fickle as well as strong. One day we waited at our William River camp for the wind to abate enough to hike to the giant dunes. We headed out when it became quieter late in the afternoon, but half way there the wind returned with a vengeance, filling the air with sand, stinging our eyes and making it difficult even to see. We had no

The William River narrows as it takes a sharp turn and sand bars accumulate along the east bank.

choice but to go back. As we neared the river, we saw that the tracks we had made only two hours earlier had been obliterated.

When the big blow continued for most of the following day, we thought we might be out of luck again. Then in the early evening the wind moderated enough for us to try once more. By the time we reached the giant dunes it was dead calm. Even when we climbed to the top of one, it was completely quiet, almost eerie. To the northwest, the low sun bathed the giants in a golden glow as they seemed to line up in formation most of the way to Lake Athabasca, visible in the distance. The winding crest of our dune flowed with intensified form and contrast as the east slope fell into shadow and the west slope turned shades of gold, then red.

We had been on top of this dune before. But something felt different this time, profoundly different, although we didn't immediately recognize what it was. The silence. The total absence of wind had created a rare place where we could experience true silence. The northern wilderness is seldom completely quiet, what with rustling leaves, trickling water, songs of birds and frogs, the buzz of mosquitoes, and strange things that go bump in the night. All of that was gone now, leaving only the twilight glow of giants and a stillness so penetrating that we were afraid that even a whisper would break the spell.

The William's complex riverbed with sand of varying depths visible below the water surface. In the lower left corner is the start of the creek which runs from the William River to the northeast part of William Point.

Butterscotch Pudding and Whipped Cream

As we neared the mouth of the William River, the huge sand dunes of the west bank gave way to forested sand hills, then to the forested lowlands of the delta. Unlike most of the other major dune fields, the William River field does not border Lake Athabasca, but is separated from it by a series of ancient beach ridges, many with peat bogs between them.

The sand-choked delta fanned into the lake. Semi-stabilized sand bars were scattered everywhere, some forming low islands where vegetation had taken hold. We were faced with a mind-boggling array of channels, none of which appeared deep enough for a canoe. Finally it was no use. We had to forget about paddling and ended up walking while trying to keep the canoe afloat in the shallow water. It was little better when we entered the lake, since the water beyond the delta was so shallow that we were forced to continue wading until we were far into Lake Athabasca.

Seeing the William River from the air was pure magic. At the end of our trip when we flew over the braided river and delta, the William was transformed into a gigantic abstract painting, in many places resembling butterscotch pudding marbled with whipped

As the William River nears Lake Athabasca it begins to widen into a delta.

cream. Multi-hued golds and beiges indicated varying depths of underwater sand bars. Above-water sand bars appeared alabaster white, deeper channels ranged from copper to chocolate brown, and suspended organic matter in the water gave the delta a purple tinge. Framing the entire painting was the vibrant green of the forest and the white slip faces of dunes dropping into the water.

The Athabasca Sand Dunes never failed to surprise, fascinate and delight us. But if we were to choose one defining experience, it would surely be the flight over the William River. It was as if we were given a second set of eyes through which another face of nature was revealed—a face of exquisite beauty, mystery and wonder.

Up the Creek

Since our first trip down the William River in 1990, we have made several canoe trips upstream as far as the last set of rapids. To avoid the sand-clogged delta, we take a short creek which branches off the William River about three kilometres from its mouth and empties into the lake on the northeast part of William Point. In years when the lake level is low, we have to wade over shallow areas at the creek mouth until we reach deeper water upstream. The concentrated flow in the narrow creek makes for a strenuous paddle against the strong current, so much so that even a slight hesitation in paddling or a stroke lost to swatting a mosquito begins to sweep us downstream. Resting means pulling into

Delta of the William River.

shore or hanging on tightly to tree branches.

The creek twists and turns as it follows a path among ancient beach ridges. It has almost a jungle-like feel to it, with both banks clothed in thick bushes. The first time we made this upstream trip, we were helped along by thoughts of how much fun it was going to be to ride the creek downstream a few days later. Little did we realize just how exciting it would be.

We drifted downstream on one of those perfect northern July days, pleasantly warm with just enough breeze to keep the mosquitoes at bay, fluffy white clouds floating in a deep blue sky, and the forest a glorious green. We had to do little but steer around the tight turns as we zipped down the narrow creek. Robin casually mentioned that the only thing missing on this most perfect of days was a bear or moose on shore to photograph as we passed by.

It was a classic case of being careful what you wish for in case your wish comes true. As we rounded the last curve of the creek and began to slow down for the sand bars near the lake, there stood a large bull moose feeding

A narrow creek extends from the William River to Lake Athabasca. The mouth of the creek, in the foreground, is very shallow.

The delta of the William River extends far into Lake Athabasca.

near the water's edge. Almost instantly we sensed that this wasn't going to be a typical wildlife sighting. Our quick and silent approach likely startled the moose, and for a second or two he stared directly at us without moving. Then he lowered his head and charged, his long legs effortlessly splashing through the shallow water.

It is quite possible that this moose had never seen people or a canoe. Aiming his head directly for the centre of the canoe, he may have regarded us as a strange two-headed intruder. There was no time to think or plan what to do. At the last second Robin swung his paddle and we heard a loud crack as it caught the moose on the end of his nose. To our surprise, he stopped and shook his head as he towered above us. We paddled furiously at a speed that would likely have qualified us for the Olympic finals, sand bars or no sand bars!

Soon we were caught in the sand-choked creek mouth and had to get out of the canoe. We looked back; the moose was still staring at us and shaking his head, but he didn't seem inclined to come after us, probably satisfied that he had driven us away.

We think about this moose each time we canoe the creek, and indeed anytime we canoe a narrow waterway anywhere in moose country. And while we still enjoy a quiet peaceful paddle, we have never been quite so quiet since.

The William River as seen from an airplane. The bottom of the picture is a sand dune on the west bank of the river. This is the same bank that appears in the photograph on pages 20-21, only here we are looking at it from directly above.

Lake Athabasca in a rare period of calm.

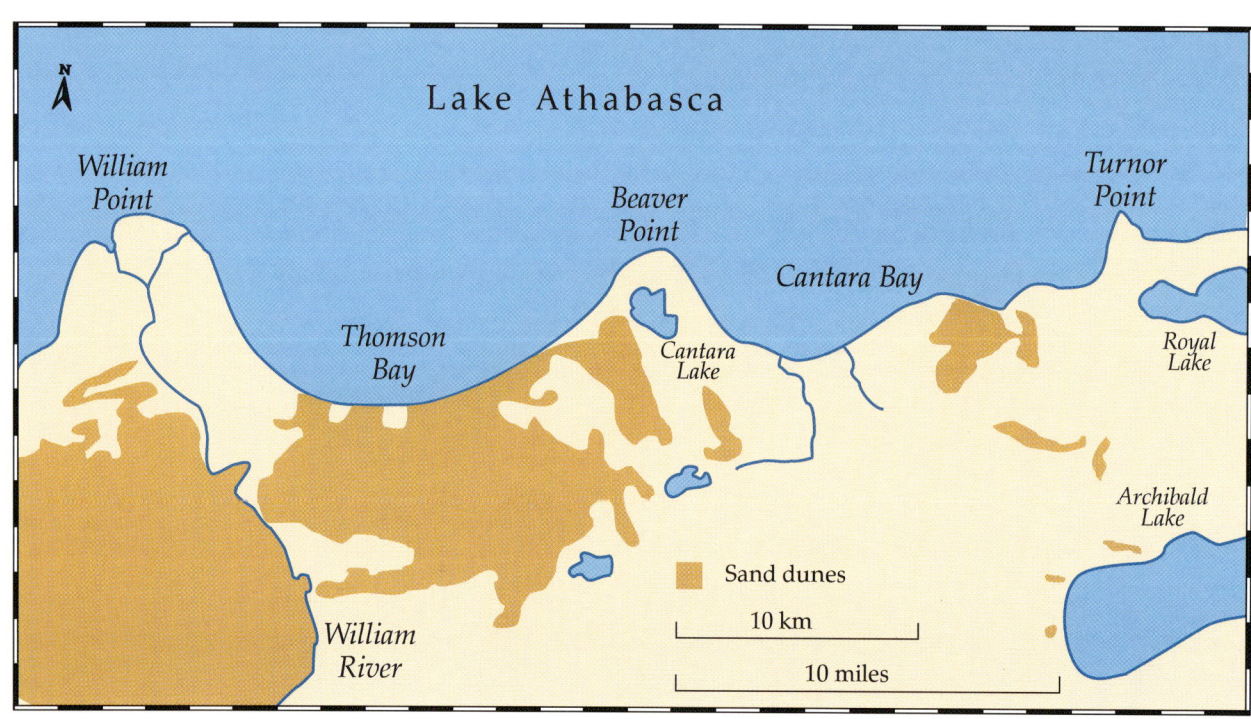

Lake Athabasca

On our first trip down the William River we were concerned that we would arrive at the lake and find conditions too rough for travel. Lake Athabasca is like an inland sea, over 280 kilometres long and covering 7,850 square kilometres. The fourth largest lake entirely within Canada, Athabasca is known for its powerful winds and fierce storms. The south shore is totally exposed to the elements with no sheltered bays or islands to provide refuge. Storms have taken their toll here; even freight barges have broken up, scattering huge timbers, steel tanks and other debris along the shore.

THOMSON BAY

To our amazement and relief, we found the lake dead calm, the satin smooth water resembling a gigantic mirror. Thin layers of clouds shrouded the distant eastern and western horizons, blending water and sky. Across the lake, the rugged north shore shimmered as a blue-gray mirage, with constantly changing raised cliffs, flat-topped buttes and anvil-shaped hills. It was an optical illusion more common to the Arctic, when hot air lies above cold air and light rays are bent, playing tricks with reality.

Rounding William Point we saw the broad smooth sweep of Thomson Bay stretching another 25 kilometres or so to Beaver Point. The deepest part of the bay was lined with sand, broken by an occasional patch of forest. Beyond it lay the immense Thomson Bay dune field, the second largest in the park, covering 97 square kilometres. The dunes extend south of the lake for about nine kilometres, with a tongue reaching as far west as the William River.

After a leisurely paddle in perfect conditions we pulled onto a wide beach backed by beach ridges, with a small attractive woodland just up the hill. We set up camp near shore and celebrated our good luck in finding such calm conditions. It seemed too good to be true. And it was.

Thomson Bay on the south shore of Lake Athabasca, with Beaver Point in the background.

About 3:00 a.m. we were awakened by howling winds, pounding waves and a pinging on our tent which sounded like rain. But it wasn't raining. We were being sandblasted! Although it was a warm night, we had to close all the vents and flaps on the tent, but to no avail. In a few hours everything was covered with a fine layer of talcum powder sand, including us.

Later that morning the wind eased and the sand stopped blowing, but the crashing waves continued unabated. It was a pattern we would see many times on this lake; once the waves gained momentum, they took a long time to settle down. We were wind-bound, or more accurately wave-bound, the first of many times during our south shore journeys. It was always difficult to plan a trip on this lake; we never knew when we might be stranded for a day, two days or a week.

Our forced layover was a blessing in disguise, allowing us to explore the area in more detail. This special spot on Thomson Bay, which we discovered quite by accident, has become one of our favorite places in the dunes, and one to which we return on every trip.

Thomson Bay is lined by a broad sandy beach, broken in only a few places where willows reach the water's edge. Just behind the beach is a series of ancient raised beaches, sometimes called fossil beaches, no longer

Many beach ridges in Thomson Bay are subject to blowouts.

subject to waves or pushing by winter ice. A few beach ridges near shore are separated by shallow lagoons, but most are dry and partially stabilized with vegetation.

These beach ridges form when the lake level lowers, allowing wind-driven waves to push up sand from the widened beach and from newly exposed offshore sand bars. Ice push also helps form the ridges, as storm winds during spring breakup drive ice masses ashore into the sand. Scientists estimate that this periodic lowering of the lake occurred on average every 30 years. In the William River delta area, where 35 beach ridges developed, the process would have taken around 1,050 years.

The sandy ridges become more stable as dune grasses, shrubs and willows take hold. Eventually, stands of white spruce populate the higher ridges. As we travelled along the south shore, most of the forest appeared to be white spruce, however it only grows in a narrow band close to the water's edge. Farther inland spruce is less prevalent, with jack pine occupying the older beach ridges and most of the forest.

Close to where we camped on Thomson Bay, the beach ridges were pock-marked with blowouts. Here the loose sand was only partially stabilized by vegetation, and the wind was able to carry away loose particles, leaving a series of bowl-shaped depressions and hummocky dune-like hills rather than well-defined ridges. In some cases, underground springs undermined the sand, adding to the hummocky effect.

ABOVE: *Bunchberries*. RIGHT: *Blowouts undermine this spruce tree, exposing its roots.*

Enchanted Forests

The forest behind our campsite was a tiny oasis, completely surrounded by sand dunes. Beach ridge blowouts extended to the edge of the forest, where towering white spruce were being undercut by the wind, some with exposed roots over two metres above ground. Farther back many spruce were draped in feathery strands of old man's beard, a delicate olive-colored lichen found mainly in mature forests. We even found old man's beard on tiny trees less than a metre high.

The hummocky forest floor had a patchwork of ground cover including reindeer lichen, kinnikinnick (common bearberry), crowberry and blueberry. Thick clusters of bunchberries grew in sheltered hollows, while other areas were blanketed in Labrador tea. The highlight was stemless ladyslippers flowering in brilliant shades of red and pink. While these showy orchids are quite common along the south shore, here they were so profuse that we constantly had to be careful where we stepped. Stemless ladyslippers flower early in the summer, reaching their peak around the end of June and early July. By mid-July, few flowers are left.

For a sweeping view of all of Thomson Bay, we climbed an immense dome-shaped

Stemless ladyslippers are common along the south shore of Lake Athabasca.

61

Spruce trees atop a sand dune in Thomson Bay. The top picture was taken in 1990, and the bottom one in 1996. Note the extent to which the roots are exposed in each picture.

dune that rises over the lake shore. Little vegetation survives here, although the odd white spruce clings tenaciously to life. Near the top of the dune we found a pair of spruce, a larger tree with a long exposed root curving a metre or so above ground, and a smaller companion resting on a platform of roots which had been partially undercut by the wind.

Each time we returned to Thomson Bay we climbed the dune to see how this isolated pair was faring, and we discovered just how quickly and dramatically the ground level can change. Four years after our first visit, the long twisted root was being reburied and the partially exposed platform of roots on the smaller tree was completely buried. Two years later,

Ripples in the sand.

much of the sand had blown away again, exposing more roots. The next year we saw even more roots as the wind continued to undermine the trees.

When we saw the changes that took place in only a few years, it became easier to appreciate the dynamic effect of moving sand over hundreds and thousands of years. Near our camp, an exhumed forest covered the slope of a dune facing the lake. Trees buried long ago by sand had been more recently exhumed from their sandy tomb as the dune advanced farther east. Now desiccated tree trunks devoid of bark protrude from the deep sand, their brittle remains often ending in needle-sharp points.

A ghostly whitish-gray by day, these ancient skeletons seemed to take on a new life as the late evening sun lingered over the lake, bathing them in a warm red glow. Massive upturned roots resembled other-worldly sea monsters standing guard over the spectral forest. From the top of the dune, the skeleton arms bent in contorted shapes, silhouetted against the fiery sun. It became our evening ritual to hike up the dune for sunset in the enchanted forest. Never did it look the same as the night before, and never did we tire of its magic.

ABOVE, LEFT, AND OVERLEAF: *Ghostly stands of exhumed trees overlooking Thomson Bay. This ancient forest, once buried by sand, has more recently been uncovered as the sand dune migrated farther east.*

Circles in the sand. The circles are created as blades of grass are whipped around by Athabasca's strong winds.

STORIES IN THE SAND

We encountered animal tracks almost everywhere we went in Thomson Bay, especially near the beach. The most artistic tracks belonged to the Canadian toad which rarely appears in the heat of the day, but crosses large expanses of sand during the cooler nights. We saw where moose wandered out of the forest, where sandhill cranes landed on the beach, and where a wolf walked near the water's edge then made a wide semicircle around our camp.

Wildlife was never far away. One day we inadvertently startled a cow moose and her calf browsing on bushes near the shore. We watched with envy at the way they ran effortlessly up a steep sand dune slope, the same slope we would trudge up slowly while huffing and puffing. One morning we noticed fresh moose tracks beside our tent, yet we had heard nothing during the night.

We saw bear tracks at the base of a dune not far from camp, and each day there were fresh signs. The bear likely knew we were there but wasn't curious enough to investigate closer, or perhaps it decided to keep its distance because of previous run-ins with people. Because of the likelihood of encountering bears, we adopted a strict routine of hanging our food containers from high tree branches for the night and whenever we were away from camp. We never had problems with bears getting into our food, although a persistent squirrel almost succeeded in gnawing through the strap of one of our hanging bags.

One hot afternoon we were eating lunch in the shade of a birch tree overlooking the broad beach when we noticed a dark shape between the hummocky ridges. We immediately assumed it was a moose or bear, but when it finally climbed to the top of a hummock about 30 metres away, there stood a woodland caribou. As soon as the magnificent dark tan-colored animal saw us, it raised its nose high in the air, then sauntered off into the forest.

Tracks in the sand.
TOP LEFT: *Black bear.*
TOP RIGHT: *Crossroads in the sand, with the larger tracks belonging to the Canadian toad.*
CENTRE LEFT: *Woodland caribou.*
CENTRE RIGHT: *A bird, likely a spruce grouse, lands on a dune then walks across the sand.*
BOTTOM LEFT: *Tracks are sometimes surprising. Here a pebble rolling down the slope of a sand bank leaves a rippling track.*

Spotted sandpiper.

This was the only time we saw a caribou on the south shore, and it turned out to be a fairly rare sighting. The woodland caribou population here is quite small, with a few around Carswell Lake, and another herd near Davy Lake along the MacFarlane River. Later at Otherside River Lodge we told local Dene guides about our sighting. Most said they have seen woodland caribou, but not often, and seldom close to the lake.

As we walked along the beach ridges and lower parts of the sand dunes, we found pieces of bleached and sandblasted caribou antlers sticking out of the sand. Until only a few decades ago, the south shore was part of the wintering grounds for barren-ground caribou which migrated here each year from their calving and grazing grounds farther north in the tundra. William Point used to be a major lake crossing for the caribou, but it hasn't been used since the mid-1950s. In recent years, the caribou have wintered between Lake Athabasca and the Northwest Territories border, rarely crossing to the south shore.

The number of tracks can give the misleading impression that the wildlife is more abundant than it actually is. In fact, scientists suggest that the density of wildlife may actually be lower than in other parts of the north, simply because sand isn't the best habitat. Unlike the plant life of Athabasca, with its unique adaptations to the dunes, the animals are fairly typical of the northern Saskatchewan boreal forest.

We saw a variety of birds along the lake. Killdeer were common in the dunes near

Old traps, long since forgotten, are still set but rusted in position.

shore, and bald eagles often flew by and landed in the tall spruce. Most days we saw common loons close to shore, silently slipping beneath the waves in search of food, or uttering their haunting cry. The stillness of the evening was often broken by the sudden loud flutter of wings as a flock of scoters gained momentum to lift off the water. Most birds that nest here are typical of the boreal forest. However, a few Arctic-nesters have also taken to the lake and sand dunes, including the semipalmated plover, red-throated loon, red-necked phalarope, least sandpiper and Arctic tern.

STORIES FROM THE PAST

Occasionally the sand told stories about people. Just behind a forested beach ridge, but well into the dunes, we came across two traps still set as if waiting for their prey, but long since rusted in position. Likely buried for many years, they were now uncovered by the moving sand. We wondered about the people who had set them. How long ago were they here? What brought them to an isolated desert-like country? And why didn't they return?

Later we told Joe Martin from Fond du Lac about the traps, and he related a story about two trappers from Uranium City who once had trap lines near the William River. It seems they were out quite late one winter

Lake Athabasca's north and south shores are dramatically different. The north shore is characterized by bays, islands, rocky outcroppings, and cliffs such as these in Reed Bay.

when one of them fell through the ice and drowned. His partner was anxious to get back to Uranium City but, as the ice was deteriorating quickly, the only way he made it was by crawling on his hands and knees part way across the huge lake to better distribute his weight. We don't know if these were his traps. If they were, we can hardly blame him for not coming back.

Archaeologists tell us that people have been coming here for close to 8,000 years. Early inhabitants were largely dependent on barren-ground caribou which migrated every year between forested wintering grounds near Lake Athabasca and calving and grazing grounds farther north on the tundra. The caribou hunt remained an essential part of the local economy well into this century.

Climatic conditions have fluctuated dramatically over the last few thousand years, causing the treeline to move north and retreat south at different times. This in turn affected caribou migration patterns and attracted people with different cultural traditions. When the climate grew colder about 3,500 years ago and the treeline retreated south, ancestors of today's Inuit moved as far south as Lake Athabasca. Archaeologists indicate that these former residents of the central Arctic became dependent on the caribou. About 2,500 years ago the climate improved, and Lake Athabasca became home to people believed to be ancestors of the Dene, formerly known as Chipewyan, who live in northern Saskatchewan today.

Lake Athabasca's south shore is known for shallow water and sandy shoals.

Archaeologists have also found that different cultures occupied the western and eastern parts of Lake Athabasca, with Thomson Bay being the approximate dividing line. People near the eastern half of the lake subsisted on caribou. Those to the west, influenced by Northern Plains cultures, also hunted bison which once populated the western end of the lake.

THE FUR TRADE

Peter Pond was the first European in the Lake Athabasca area. In 1778 he set up a fur trading post on the Athabasca River just south of the west end of Lake Athabasca. Here he had access to both Cree and Chipewyan territories, and over the next few years accumulated an enormous number of furs which he took east to market. Pond may have explored part of the lake in 1783, although it is unclear if he travelled along the south shore as far as the sand dunes.

The first person to write about the dunes was Philip Turnor, surveyor for the Hudson's Bay Company. The Bay was concerned that the rival Northwest Company was taking trade goods directly to the Chipewyan of the Athabasca country and cutting into its business. Turnor was engaged to find out more about Athabasca and how best to conduct trade, and to investigate rumors that Athabasca might be close to the Pacific Ocean. With assistant Peter Fidler and others, Turnor explored the lake in 1791.

Turnor's journal is sparse on details about the south shore, but near the William River and Thomson Bay he refers to "a rising sandy desert of a yellowish white Colour with a chance scub pine standing singly..." [sic]. Turnor must have been impressed by the dune scenery as he sprinkled personal comments into his straightforward, business-like writing. Home sickness may have struck when he reached the dunes next to the MacFarlane River, which he described as "fields of ripe corn between ledges of woods such as are seen in the Hill countrys of England" [sic].

A century passed before anyone wrote about the dunes again. Joseph Burr Tyrrell and D.B. Dowling travelled Athabasca's south shore in 1892 and reported on the area for the Geological Survey of Canada. Their report notes that "sand hills rise in some cases nearly a hundred feet above the general level." The William River was described as falling "in short cascades over beds of sandstone." Tyrrell named the hills inland from the south shore the "Fish Mountains or Hills", and described the waterfalls, rapids and gorge on the MacFarlane River, known then as the Beaver River.

The west end of Lake Athabasca was a hub of activity during the fur trade. Fort Chipewyan, founded in 1788, soon became known as the Emporium of the North, one of the most prominent posts of the fur trade era. Most traders came by way of the famous Methye Portage near present-day La Loche, Saskatchewan. Here they could cross a 21-kilometre height of land which joined the Churchill and Saskatchewan River systems that flowed into Hudson Bay with the Clearwater and Athabasca Rivers that flowed to the Arctic.

David Thompson reached the east end of Lake Athabasca in 1796 by way of Reindeer Lake and Wollaston Lake, as part of an effort by the Hudson's Bay Company to find a shorter route to Athabasca. Both the Hudson's Bay Company and the Northwest Company set up posts near the eastern side of the lake but they were short-lived, never matching the popularity of Fort Chipewyan. It wasn't until 1851 that the Hudson's Bay Company established a permanent trading post at Fond du Lac. Today, Fond du Lac is the largest Saskatchewan community on Lake Athabasca, home to about 1,000 residents.

Remarkably little was known about the sand dunes until scientific studies began in the early 1900s. But perhaps this is only remarkable from today's perspective. Most modern visitors appreciate the dunes as a visual treat or a scientific curiosity. To people preoccupied with the day-to-day challenge of making a living from hunting, trapping, or fishing, there were simply more productive areas around Lake Athabasca.

Perhaps the sand dunes were also ignored because of the lack of safe anchorages. Unlike the island-studded north shore with its deep bays and sheltered coves, the south shore along the sand dunes is completely exposed to the elements, with no islands or protected bays to wait out a storm. Combine this with Athabasca's famous winds, shallow water and sandy shoals that extend far into the lake, and the south shore may not have looked all that attractive to early visitors.

Nevertheless, a few people from communities such as Fond du Lac, Camsell Portage and Fort Chipewyan used the south shore and built cabins in the woodlands and along the small lakes adjoining the dunes. Almost all are gone now. One cabin belongs to Joe Martin from Fond du Lac. He still runs a trap line near

The abandoned Gunnar mine on Lake Athabasca's north shore.

Royal Lake, and takes his family there each year for part of the winter. Traditional aboriginal use of the land is allowed to continue in the provincial park.

BOOM AND BUST

Most of Lake Athabasca's recent history was played out on the north shore, almost directly across the lake from the sand dunes. Here mining communities flourished then died. Goldfields was established in the 1930s after the discovery of gold. Its heyday was brief, as a shortage of manpower and materials during World War II, combined with increasing costs to extract the low grade ore, led to the mine closure. Goldfields came to life again for a short time in the 1940s when it served as an exploration base for uranium. In 1952, the exodus to the new town of Uranium City began and Goldfields was soon abandoned.

Not far away, on the southern edge of the Crackingstone Peninsula, Gunnar boomed after uranium was discovered in 1952. The community developed rapidly, with a grocery store, butcher shop, beauty parlor, post office, bank, hospital and curling rink. The mine closed in 1964 when reserves were exhausted. Today Gunnar is a ghost town of ruined buildings with creaking doors, half-submerged

OVERLEAF: *Looking northwest from Cantara Bay towards Beaver Point. Just inland is tiny Cantara Lake and a series of ancient beach ridges.*

Stones cover the beach at Beaver Point.

docks, derelict towers and an enormous flooded hole that was once the open pit mine.

Uranium City lasted longest and thrived for almost 30 years. But here too, uranium reserves were eventually depleted. In 1981 when Eldorado Nuclear announced that the mine would close the following year, Uranium City was home to 3,000 people. Now about 200 live here.

During Uranium City's boom years, the sand dunes became better known when residents boated across the lake to explore this strange, other-worldly landscape so close to home. Concern for the fragile nature of the area grew when all-terrain vehicles left permanent marks in the desert pavement. Ironically, the tragedy of Uranium City's demise contributed to the preservation of the sand dunes: depopulation meant less human pressure.

While the special nature of the dunes had been recognized for some time, it wasn't until the 1970s that the Saskatchewan government proposed formal protection. A Crown Reserve established in 1973 prevented further mineral exploration. In 1988 Athabasca Sand Dunes Park Land Reserve was designated, then after four years of public consultation, Athabasca Sand Dunes Provincial Wilderness Park was declared in 1992.

Slip face of a sand dune in Cantara Bay.

Pink Clouds and Warm Breezes

Beaver Point lies at the eastern end of Thomson Bay, dominated by a high hill which is one of the south shore's most recognizable landmarks. Behind the hill is tiny Cantara Lake, less than a kilometre away along an old portage trail. The lake is sometimes used as a drop-off and pick-up point by visitors, since float planes can usually land here when conditions are too rough on Lake Athabasca.

We once met a group of hikers who had come from Fort Smith, Northwest Territories, only about 200 kilometres away by air. A float plane had dropped them at Cantara Lake. From there they walked along the beach of Thomson Bay, then across the Thomson Bay dune field to where it touches the William River. After wading across the river, they hiked to the giant dunes. We met them on their way back to Cantara Lake where the float plane was scheduled to return the next day. While we still preferred travelling by canoe, we envied their not having to worry about Lake Athabasca's wild mood swings.

The first thing we noticed at Beaver Point was the stones. Along the sand-choked braided section of the William River and the beach in Thomson Bay, we saw no stones at all. We were hard pressed even to find a pebble. There the underlying sandstone formation is covered in a thick layer of sand, but near Beaver Point the sandstone formation is much closer to the surface. Rounded boulders poke through the sand, polished smooth by wind and waves, and evenly spaced as if someone had laid down paving stones.

What concerned us most about Beaver Point were the sand bars extending far into the lake and the high waves breaking over them. We had to travel around the bars, then turn right into Cantara Bay while being hit broadside by the waves.

When wind continues throughout the day, it is sometimes possible to find a relatively calm period in late evening. Sometimes is the key word: Lake Athabasca tends to do what it likes, when it likes! We waited out the weather near Beaver Point, then decided to press on when the waves calmed down somewhat around 10:00 p.m., still quite light in mid-summer. We rounded the point and fought the waves without taking on too much water and started into Cantara Bay as conditions continued to improve. Soon it calmed down completely and we thought that this was our chance to make up for lost time. But around midnight, when rolling swells began to build, we decided to stop and make camp.

Scattered dune fields lie south of Cantara Bay, with the largest one extending to the lake shore. In places the slip faces of dunes have advanced over thinly treed, grass covered plains. Another flat sandy plain has several scattered boulders. Parts of the beach are covered in small flat stones, with a few widely spaced trees.

While Thomson Bay was one big crescent-shaped curve, the shoreline from Cantara Bay to the mouth of the MacFarlane River was a series of shallow bays, broken by sand bars and sandy points jutting into the lake. The biggest of these was Turnor Point, named after early Hudson's Bay Company surveyor Philip Turnor.

Winds from the northwest and northeast are the norm, but one summer we had strong southeast winds that lasted several days. After a hot spell, the temperature cooled and it felt refreshing as we paddled along the south shore. But every time we came near a dune field, the southeast wind would sweep across

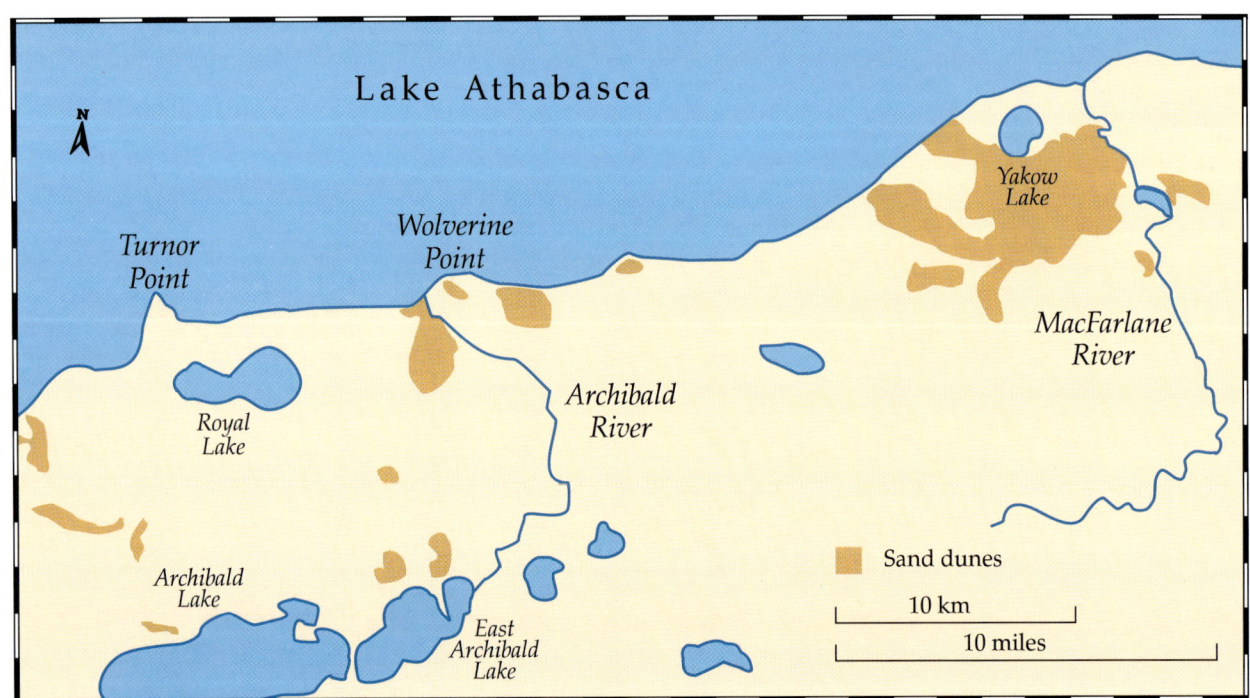

Dune field in Cantara Bay.

the still warm sand and hit us with a blast that seemed like it was coming from a forced air furnace.

Not all of the dune fields extend to the water's edge, but sometimes we could tell where they were by simply looking at the sky. The clouds often had a pinkish tinge, even at midday. The phenomenon was strongest in storm clouds which reflected like a beacon, at once both inviting and eerie.

Archibald River

The Archibald River was a delight to explore. The smallest river in the park, it originates in East Archibald Lake, only 12 kilometres inland, and picks up additional flow from Wilson Creek about five kilometres upstream from Lake Athabasca. Although a small river, it carries on average 11 tonnes of sand per day into the lake. Just 10 metres wide and a metre or so deep, the Archibald is hidden beneath a high mixed forest canopy for most of its length. But for the last two to three kilometres before reaching Lake Athabasca, the west bank of the narrow river is dwarfed by massive dunes over 30 metres high.

We landed at a narrow tongue of the five square kilometre dune field which extends close to the lake's edge, about 500 metres west of the river mouth. The narrow beach ridge

ABOVE: *Early morning fog on Lake Athabasca.* LEFT: *A cliff of fractured sandstone on the shore of Lake Athabasca near the Archibald River.*

between the shore and slip face of the dune was like a manicured park, with birch, jack pine, and felt-leaved willow evenly spaced as if they were planted. Scattered among them were various shrubs, sprigs of wild raspberries, and splashes of color from fireweed and wild roses.

The gently curved beach was covered in smooth flat stones of every size, from heavy slabs to thin pieces with rounded edges that fit into the palm of your hand. This was a stone skipper's paradise, with an endless supply of stones tailor-made for bouncing across the water. As it turned out we would have plenty of time to practise our stone skipping skills.

Before deciding where to set up camp we checked the area for shorebirds, since some species favor pebbly beaches for nest sites. The rare piping plover, usually found much farther south, was spotted here several years ago and may nest in the area. But we saw no sign of nesting shorebirds. Had there been nests on the stony beach earlier in the summer, they surely would have been washed away by the high lake level and storm waves.

Just west of the beach, a small cliff of beautiful multi-colored fractured sandstone lies exposed on the water's edge, with chunks of flagstone-like rocks strewn around its base. The cliff is part of a fault line in the underlying sandstone formation which rises like a step at the edge of the lake. While the cliff extends along the lake shore, this is one of the few places where the bedrock is exposed rather

Reindeer lichen blankets much of the forest floor in the Athabasca Sand Dunes.

than covered by sand or vegetation.

Even ancient beach ridges here are made of stone, looking like narrow paved roads running through the bush from the foot of the dune near our camp to the mouth of the river. In some places it seemed as if the flat stones had been deliberately inlaid like paving blocks, while in others the thickly piled loose stones clattered as if we were walking on broken glass.

Elements of forest, meadows, wetlands and dunes came together in this little beach ridge area, sandwiched between the lake and the steep slip face of the dune. Brilliant yellow blossoms of Indian tansy contrasted with magenta fireweed, blue-violet harebells, and the deep pink of prickly rose bushes.

A female spruce grouse wandered across the stone beach ridge, apparently unconcerned that we were so close. She quietly went about her business foraging in the vegetation, and was soon joined by two tiny chicks. We watched them for several minutes until they made their way into thicker bushes.

Moose and bear tracks were common, so we weren't surprised when we woke up one morning to find fresh bear tracks about 10 metres from the tent. The bear had come down from the hill that rises over the sandstone cliff, probably with the intention of walking along the shore towards the river mouth. The tracks told us that the bear had stopped abruptly, likely when it saw our tent, then made a 90-degree turn and climbed the sand dune in order to avoid us. The next morning we noticed fresh moose tracks about

The Archibald River is dwarfed by towering sand dunes on its west bank and tall forest on its east bank.

Archibald River.

the same distance away, only this time the widely spaced tracks revealed that the moose had run once it saw our camp.

The area around our campsite felt familiar yet strange. On a previous trip, when the lake level was much lower, we had to drag our canoe over sand bars stretching the entire length of the beach in order to reach shore. Then the beach was also wide enough that we could easily walk to the sandstone cliff. Three years later the shoreline had changed dramatically. The water was so high that the sand bars had completely disappeared, the stony beach was much narrower, and the only way we could reach the sandstone cliff was by canoe.

The slip face of the dune was only a few steps from our lake shore campsite, but once we climbed on top it was a different world. The sand extended back from the lake as far as we could see, mottled with sections of desert pavement. Unlike the monotone desert pavement near the William River, these stones had an orange tinge. Geologists attribute the color to minerals from groundwater adhering to the stones.

Little vegetation covered the sand, other than clumps of sea lyme-grass, other dune grasses and the odd birch tree clinging stubbornly to life. Clumps of exhumed forest along with charred remains of trees destroyed in forest fires lay scattered about. Scientists believe that this dune field is not as old as some of the

Lake Athabasca's stone-covered beach near the mouth of the Archibald River is constantly being reworked by powerful waves.

others, and that it formed when fires cleared parts of the forest, allowing blowouts to start which eventually grew into dunes.

Our main reason for travelling here was to see the dramatic dunes that rise above the river. The forces at work are similar to those at the William River, as the prevailing northwesterly winds relentlessly push sand across the dune field and down the steep slip faces into the river. But the Archibald's setting is even more impressive, with the tiny river almost lost in a deep canyon of towering dunes on one side and thick stands of mature tall black spruce on the other.

On one curve in the river where the sand was more stable than elsewhere, the steep bank was peppered with holes made by a colony of nesting bank swallows. The golden sand was alive with activity as the adults darted in and out to catch insects and feed their young. We had to be careful to stay well away from the crest of this dune; even the slightest disturbance could collapse the precarious nesting colony.

Almost every day we heard the throaty gurgling call of sandhill cranes flying over the river mouth and landing in the dune field. We often came across fresh crane tracks and could easily see where they landed, where they walked and where they took off again.

Ancient stone beach ridge near the mouth of the Archibald River.

Stranded

On our most recent trip we had planned a short stay of a couple days or so near the Archibald River. We were there for seven. After two days of near dead calm conditions on the lake, the waves began. First brought on by powerful winds, they intensified as a series of thunderstorms passed through. Even after the winds died, pounding waves continued to batter the shore.

The waves would begin breaking on one end of the curved beach, then barrel along its length with the sound of thunder. Each wave grasped all the flat stones it could hold then tossed them about wildly. As our tent was less than 10 metres from shore, the noise of the roar and clattering stones became so intense that we had to shout to hear each other. During our week-long stay we watched the beach being dramatically reworked, with the waves coming first from the northeast, then the northwest, then again from the northeast.

Like other places where we had been stranded on the south shore, being windbound here was no great hardship as there was plenty of fascinating country to explore. In fact, a longer stay encouraged us to look beyond the obvious. Besides the eastern edge of the dune field along the river, we also ventured farther into the western fringes of the dune field where it meets the forest.

From a distance it looked as if the sand simply ended and the forest began, but as we got closer we saw that there was more of a transition area. The edge of the jack pine and

Archibald River.

birch forest was interspersed with clearings where blowouts had created active sand dunes. Walking to the end of a blowout, we would often find an entrance to another clearing with more blowouts and dunes. It was like a series of doorways into hidden sandy worlds that took us deeper and deeper into the forest. One shallow bowl-shaped clearing about a hundred metres across was pure sand. The only intrusion into the smooth bowl was a symmetrical cluster of bright flowering fireweed, looking as if someone had planted a flower pot.

At the edge of the dune field above the sandstone cliff we found shallow but distinct beach ridges composed of mostly flat pebbles. These ridges ran at a different angle than the lower beach ridges next to the shore, and were from a time when the lake was much higher and the waves hit the shore from a different direction.

A consolation of being storm-stayed was the fishing. We had not even tried fishing since leaving Carswell Lake, because the sandy conditions along the William River and Lake Athabasca's south shore make for poor

A birch tree with exposed roots sits atop a sand dune overlooking Lake Athabasca near the mouth of the Archibald River.

fish habitat. Here, however, we could wander down to the mouth of the Archibald River around 11:00 a.m. and be quite confident of having a fair sized northern pike for lunch.

Just as the waves were beginning to build one evening, we watched a motor boat slowly approach from the western horizon, then pull into the mouth of the river. This is one of the few places along the south shore where travellers can take a motor boat into protected waters without having to haul it ashore, but only in years when the lake level is unusually high.

Soon after, our new neighbors walked over to introduce themselves. Rod and Caron used to live in Uranium City, and every summer they return to Lake Athabasca. "We keep coming back for obvious reasons," said Rod as he looked over the beautiful setting. As in previous summers, they and their five kids were spending a couple weeks cruising around Lake Athabasca, stopping to camp at some of the most gorgeous spots in the north.

They were storm-bound as well, but like us they found no shortage of things to do—hiking in the dunes, exploring the forest, fishing, swimming in the shallow sandy river during the hot weather. The kids revelled in the freedom of a gigantic summer playground.

Over many cups of tea we swapped stories about our Athabasca travels. We enjoyed getting the perspective of locals who knew the country much better than we could ever hope to, and who appreciated it so much that they returned every summer. Not surprisingly, we were drawn to Lake Athabasca for similar reasons—the beauty and uniqueness of the sand

The desert pavement near the Archibald River has an orange tinge caused by minerals in the groundwater. This area is covered by shallow beach ridges from a time when the lake level was much higher.

dunes, the dramatic contrast between the lake's north and south shores, and especially that rare feeling of having an enormous piece of spectacular wilderness practically all to yourself.

Most evenings we climbed the big dune behind our camp to watch the sun set over the lake. Behind us stretched the pure sand of the dune field, broken by ghostly stands of exhumed trees that took on the reddish-orange glow of the low sun. To the east, far below the slip face of the dune, was the mouth of the Archibald River, the sandy shoreline and the forest of Wolverine Point. To the west, a series of shallow bays stretched to the horizon, with Turnor Point jutting far into the lake. Over 30 kilometres away to the north, we could barely make out the high hills and cliffs of Athabasca's rugged north shore. The sun set in the northwest, becoming a huge orange ball as it dipped slowly into the widest part of the lake, saturating the water with color. The clouds glowed with hues of gold, pink and crimson, changing to an intense red which lasted until well after midnight.

As we lingered on top of the dune, it became clear that we were drawn here by much more than scenic beauty or the many scientific reasons why this land is unique. It was the larger experience, the privilege of living an ordinary day in an extraordinary place. Rod's first explanation of coming here "for obvious reasons" seemed to sum it up best.

ABOVE: *Slip face of a sand dune encroaches upon the forest floor near the Archibald River.*

OPPOSITE PAGE: *A variety of wildflowers adds color to a small forested area sandwiched between the slip face of a dune and the beach near the Archibald River.*

TOP LEFT: *Harebells*
TOP RIGHT: *Indian tansy*
BOTTOM LEFT: *Fireweed*
BOTTOM RIGHT: *Prickly rose*

MacFarlane River

We left the Archibald River and rounded Wolverine Point, a headland with sand accumulations reaching far into the lake. Another dune field lay just beyond, but we decided not to explore it. The sand didn't quite extend to the water's edge, and the shoreline was such a tangled mass of willows and bush that landing would have been difficult.

Canoeing was fairly straightforward for the next 20 kilometres or so. The scenery changed little as we passed a series of shallow bays, mostly lined with beaches with a backdrop of raised beach ridges and forest covered hills. Only isolated patches of active sand dunes came close to the lake.

Far in the distance we could see a short stretch of sand breaking the continuous green line of the shore. When we arrived and climbed the low sand ridge near shore, we saw that this was a narrow tongue of the Yakow Lake/MacFarlane River dune field. Covering 49 square kilometres and extending all the way to the MacFarlane River, this is the third largest dune field in the park and the most easterly.

Just inland is Yakow Lake, an oval-shaped lake less than two kilometres across, bordered on one side by the dune field. The dunes near the lake are coalescing as the series of individual dune ridges gradually overtake each other, filling the vegetated valleys with sand.

Despite Lake Athabasca's unpredictable moods, a comforting aspect of our canoe trip was that we were seldom far from a sandy beach to pull into and make camp at the first sign of bad weather or big waves. That was

TOP: *This rock on the beach of Lake Athabasca has ripple marks, formed by the action of wind and water. The process took place over one billion years ago when the sand that was deposited later hardened into Athabasca sandstone.*
BOTTOM: *Moving ice during spring breakup turned stones on this beach on end, forcing them into the sand.*

The MacFarlane River twists and turns just before emptying into Lake Athabasca.

about to change. From the tongue of the Yakow dunes to the mouth of the MacFarlane River, the familiar beach was replaced with almost six kilometres of low-lying land lined with willows where landing would have been, at the least, very inconvenient. As the lake level was high, even the river mouth was not readily apparent. Unlike the William River with its massive delta fanning into the lake, the mouth of the larger and deeper MacFarlane River blended into the shoreline.

The weather was worsening, with wind and waves building as we finally caught sight of the entrance to the river. An unwritten law of canoeing says that when you have to get somewhere fast, a headwind is practically guaranteed. And sure enough, the southeast wind funneled along the river, blasting us head-on. At one point the power of the wind and current matched the force of our frantic paddle strokes and we were at a standstill, the canoeing equivalent of spinning our tires. Finally the trees and river bank offered some protection and a chance to rest. We felt the same mix of emotions every time we finished a canoe trip on Lake Athabasca—sadness to leave the lake but relief to be off it.

Land of the Giant Beaver

The largest and longest river in the park, the MacFarlane carries some 11,000 tonnes of sand per day into Lake Athabasca. Considered among the north's top whitewater canoeing adventures, the MacFarlane starts about 160

MacFarlane River and the adjoining dune field.

kilometres to the south and cuts through a rugged landscape with many canyons, powerful rapids and waterfalls.

The river has been known by many names. In the journal of his 1791 trip, Hudson's Bay Company surveyor Philip Turnor said that the local Chipewyan called it the Great Beaver or Giant Beaver River. Turnor told of the legend of a species of giant beaver which turned up all the sand, as well as "Giant Indians" who killed the beaver and also became extinct.

Turnor's assistant, Peter Fidler, who spent the following year with the Chipewyan, called it the Black River and added that it was part of a travel route between Lake Athabasca and Ile-à-la-Crosse on the Churchill River. A century later, J.B. Tyrrell explored the area for the Geological Survey of Canada. He heard it called the Beaver River and the Grand Rapid River.

Our final destination was another seven kilometres upstream on the MacFarlane River, where it widens into a small lake two kilometres long and less than a kilometre wide. Forest lined both banks of the river as we paddled upstream, except for one sweeping curve where the west bank was solid sand, part of the dune field which extends northwest to Yakow Lake and Lake Athabasca.

From our campsite we could see most of the small lake with its tiny islands, fingers of rapids flowing through the willows, and forested banks. The western end of the lake was bordered by a sand dune with a huge blowout in the centre, while the eastern shore

ABOVE: *Arctic tern.* ABOVE RIGHT: *Bald eagle.* BELOW RIGHT: *Spruce grouse.*

was lined with a high steep cliff of white sandstone. To the south, the river valley disappeared into the dark green forest, accentuated by a large sand dune high in the hills. Our view changed with the weather and the light, especially in the evening as the sandstone cliff took on the glow of the setting sun.

Each time we stayed at the small lake we met other people. This part of the Athabasca Sand Dunes sees the most visitors, usually people from Fond du Lac, only 50 kilometres away by boat, who occasionally come to fish or hunt. We also met canoeists finishing trips down the MacFarlane River. They were often exhilarated from the challenging wilderness trip, but exhausted from the lengthy portage just upstream from here.

One time we were just getting settled in camp when a canoe appeared from upstream. It was a couple from Germany, perhaps in their late fifties or early sixties. They had started their journey at Fort McMurray, Alberta, paddled down the Athabasca River to the west end of Lake Athabasca, then along the south shore, stopping at the various dune fields along the way. They had a folding canoe which they could take as luggage on airplanes, and were heavily loaded for their six-week trip with food staples that consisted mostly of spaghetti and canned corned beef.

The most amazing thing about the couple, apart from their odd diet, was their love of the wilderness. This was their twenty-fourth summer in northern Canada. Every year they canoe in the Northwest Territories, Manitoba or Saskatchewan, and have probably paddled

more northern rivers than many Canadians could even name. They were surprised when we told them we were from Saskatchewan, as they said they rarely meet Canadians on their journeys. It was a reaction we often hear from Europeans—amazement that more Canadians don't enjoy or appreciate their spectacular wilderness.

This little lake is one of the best places in the park to see wildlife. The shallow willow-lined shore is perfect moose habitat. We've seen at least one moose on each visit and have come across their tracks everywhere. Early one morning we were jolted awake by a tremendous racket of splashing and grunting. We jumped out of our tent to investigate and saw two moose swimming by, grunting as they passed. Arriving at the opposite bank, they effortlessly climbed the steep dune, stood dripping and shaking the water off their dark coats, then disappeared into the forest.

Bears are common as well. Once we were paddling near the sandstone cliff when we spotted a cinnamon-colored black bear at the water's edge. The moment he saw us he started clambering straight up the steep slope, in spite of having one injured leg that seemed to be of little use. In no way did he want anything to do with us.

Every day we saw Arctic terns performing intricate aerial manoeuvres over the shallow water as they watched and dived for fish. Just after sunset when the wind had calmed, they would often gather in large numbers right in front of our campsite where flying insects were plentiful. Silently they went after the insects, swooping back and forth just above the water with graceful ballet-like moves.

We even saw wildlife right in camp. A family of spruce grouse that lived about 10

Sand dunes here are coalescing, gradually overtaking each other and filling the vegetated valleys with sand. Lake Athabasca is at the top, Yakow Lake is to the right. A series of ancient beach ridges covers the area between the two lakes.

Waterfall, MacFarlane River.

metres behind our tent was so quiet that we didn't even know about them until the second day. On our first night in camp, we were just drifting off to sleep when we heard a loud rustle at the door of our tent. We peered through the screen and discovered a frog sitting on the ground sheet, lying in wait to gobble up insects that congregated between the main part of the tent and the fly. It stayed there most of the night, usually motionless, but every so often catching another unsuspecting bug. The same pattern continued for the next three nights as the frog moved in soon after we got settled. It was like having our own personal guard frog.

The wildlife highlight was watching the bald eagles. Throughout our travels on Lake Athabasca we saw eagles in many places, but nothing like the numbers at this little lake. We sat for hours just watching them soar high above the cliffs, riding the thermals. One day we counted 20 in the air at once and we knew there were many more downstream. Occasionally two juvenile eagles would lock their talons in mid-air, free-falling briefly before separating and climbing back up on another favorable air current.

It was the abundance of fish that attracted the eagles, especially near the shallow rapids that spread into the small lake. This is probably the best fishing spot in the park with northern pike weighing as much as 15 kilograms. We could usually count on catching a fish for supper, always hoping that we wouldn't snag one of those monsters.

Waterfall, MacFarlane River.

WATERFALLS AND PICKUP STICKS

We couldn't travel any farther upstream by canoe. Just south of the small lake, the river's almost constant rapids cut through a deep valley lined in places with rocky ledges and canyons. Beyond the rapids, about six kilometres upstream, the river plunges over a series of beautiful waterfalls. This stretch of river is not in the provincial park but is part of one of the Fond du Lac Indian Reserves. No one lives here, and the entire area is pristine.

The only way we could see the falls was to hike, but we discovered that getting there wasn't easy. We couldn't follow the river because the banks were lined with boggy terrain that eventually led into a narrow canyon. We took a circuitous route, heading southwest into the forest and dune fields, then following the high ridges which offered spectacular views over the valley. The most challenging stretch was part of an area destroyed by a forest fire in 1984 that left fallen trees haphazardly strewn like pickup sticks and a vigorous growth of new trees crowded so close together that they formed an almost impenetrable wall.

We couldn't see the falls because they were hidden behind tall trees on the river's edge. We found them by following the increasing roar as we made our way through the forest. When we finally arrived we knew that the arduous hike had been worth it.

Sandstone cliffs lining a small lake on the MacFarlane River glow with the color of twilight.

The falls were spread along a kilometre or so of the river, and each set was different. In one place the river widened as it poured over the jagged bedrock, roaring through the centre but looking more delicate near the east bank as it dropped over a series of ledges. At another waterfall the river plunged over a high ledge extending from one bank to the other, loudly battering massive boulders at the base. As we sat on the rocky outcropping on the west bank and watched the river, we enjoyed the cool spray that filled the air, providing welcome relief on a hot day.

After an all too short stay at the falls, we had to begin the long hike back in order to reach camp before dark. We returned just as the sun disappeared behind the hills, totally exhausted and thinking of nothing more than sleep. As we prepared to crawl into the tent, the sandstone cliffs began to glow from the setting sun, but this time the combination of clouds and light had turned the hills and water a brilliant crimson. Forgetting about our exhaustion, we sat there and watched for close to an hour. Sleep would wait. The land of the giant beaver was weaving its magic.

Photographing the Dunes

***D**esert-like sand dunes. Unspoiled forest. Pristine wilderness lakes and rivers. Each has its own appeal for the photographer, but in the Athabasca Sand Dunes all these elements come together in a harmony of forest, water, sand and sky that practically begs to be photographed.*

Photographing this special landscape helps to focus your attention and better appreciate its many subtleties. You begin to notice more of the patterns in the sand, the textures of the desiccated wood in an ancient exhumed forest, the transition from one hue to another in underwater sand ripples in the William River. Looking through a macro lens brings to life the miniature flowers on the sea thrift and the sticky hairlike tentacles on the sundew. By observing closely, you can't help but become more curious about the forces at work here—why a dune is shaped a particular way, how a lone tree manages to survive atop a large dune, why one beach is full of rocks while another doesn't have a single pebble.

Above all, photography helps you to appreciate the dune environment as a place of beauty. The wild and unique patterns of Athabasca compel you not only to document the landscape but also to create personal interpretations of what you see, feel and experience.

Of Sun and Sand

A long-held "rule" of landscape photography is that you should do most of your shooting as close as possible to sunrise and sunset. Nowhere is that more true than in sandy environments. The bright white glare of sand on a sunny summer's day lasts from mid-morning to early evening. In early July sunrise comes before 4:00 a.m. and sunset isn't until 10:30 p.m. This doesn't mean you can't photograph in the middle of the day, but the contrast

Sand bar, William River.

between bright sand and green vegetation, for example, is more of a challenge. Midday was our time to relax. That's when we usually had our main meal since there was plenty of time to cook, and often time to sit in the shade and read our books, or have a siesta. Some days were so hot that wandering across sand dunes in mid-afternoon didn't seem appealing.

The long evenings were perfect for photography. The sun took its time dipping towards the horizon, flooding the landscape with warm light that lasted much longer than farther south. What we noticed most was the quality of that light, with a crystal clarity that is increasingly rare in many parts of the world.

The wild card in photography here, as in most places in the north, is forest fires. Even when fires are far away, heavy smoke can blanket the air for days. We have been fortunate on most of our visits, but one morning we emerged from our tent in Thomson Bay to find smoke so thick that we could barely see a kilometre down the shore. We learned later that the smoke had come from fires in northern Manitoba, several hundred kilometres away, thanks to a southeast wind. It dissipated

A rainbow over Lake Athabasca is transformed as a storm passes through.

in a few days but in the meantime we weren't able to do much photography. We were glad we had planned a long enough trip.

Equipment

We had to be completely self-sufficient for three weeks or more at a time in the wilderness. Since space was at a premium, we had to be selective with photo gear. We always carried two 35mm cameras. On our most recent trip we took a Nikon F90x and a Nikon 801s. For the majority of shots, we used a 28-70mm zoom or 80-200mm zoom lens. Other lenses we usually took included a 24mm, 50mm macro, 50mm f1.4, and a 300mm f4 lens with a 1.4 teleconverter. On some trips we also carried a Pentax 67 medium format camera with 90mm and 200mm lenses. The other essential piece of equipment was our Manfrotto 055 tripod equipped with a ball and socket head and quick release plates.

For most photographs we had the luxury of taking our time and waiting for the right light. For the aerial shots, however, we had to work quickly under a variety of weather and light conditions.

Two essentials for aerial photography include an aircraft window that opens and a good pilot. We were fortunate to have both. Flying an Otter, our pilot Cliff Blackmur was adept at getting us in position for aerial shots.

OVERLEAF: *Ancient beach ridges near the mouth of the MacFarlane River. The ridges were formed by the periodic lowering of the lake level and by isostatic rebound, the gradual uplifting of the land.*

The changing light can make a dramatic difference in the Athabasca Sand Dunes. Here, a window of light between storm clouds highlights the forest on the east bank of the William River. Near the top is a steep game trail used by wildlife to gain access to the river.

Usually he had the additional challenge of flying with a canoe strapped to one pontoon of the plane.

From the air we used a 28-70mm zoom and a 50mm f1.4 lens. While a zoom definitely allowed more creativity on the fly, we opted for the faster lens on recent trips, because it was possible to shoot at a much faster speed to compensate for the inevitable bumps in the flight. We used a polarizing filter for many aerial shots, such as those of the William River, which helped cut through glare on the water surface.

The main challenge to photography in this environment is the extremely fine sand that gets in everything, including your camera gear, no matter how careful you are. Even when there is no wind (not that often), just walking across the sand raises powder-fine grains in the air. It's best to get in the habit of putting your camera back in the bag immediately after you use it, rather than walking long distances carrying it unprotected.

Tripods really take a beating; they are exposed to the elements most of the time and the legs often stand in the sand. After every trip we have to give our tripod a thorough cleaning, taking apart all the legs and clips. Despite our best efforts, it's never been the same since the first trip.

Visiting the Athabasca Sand Dunes

The Athabasca Sand Dunes are remote, a true wilderness with no road access, services, communities or residents. Independent trips require careful planning and knowledge of wilderness camping. Travellers have to be totally self-sufficient, as well as aware of the fragile nature of the environment.

The two main canoe routes entering the park are the William and MacFarlane Rivers. Both are excellent wilderness trips, but very different. The MacFarlane is more a whitewater adventure, with rugged scenery including canyons, rapids and waterfalls. However, you will only see the sand dunes near the end of the trip. Starting points for the MacFarlane River include Brudell Lake, about 120 kilometres south of Lake Athabasca, or the Snare River which empties into the MacFarlane. These put-in points are reached by float plane.

If you're mainly interested in the sand dunes, the William is the better choice. Two options for put-in points include Carswell Lake, as described in this book, or Hale Lake which is farther upstream on the William River. Both lakes can be reached by float plane (check with provincial authorities on the current status of road access to Carswell Lake). The length of time required to canoe the William will depend on water levels and your canoeing party's whitewater experience. The water is usually higher earlier in the season because of spring run-off. In low water years more shallow rock gardens will be exposed. The Carswell Lake option may be less appealing in low water years because of the shallow nature of the Carswell River. Call the Saskatchewan Environment and Resource Management office in Stony Rapids well ahead of your intended trip for information on expected water levels.

The William River itself is only one aspect of the experience. You should allow enough time to camp along the river and hike into the

Camping in Thomson Bay.

dunes. Personally, we would consider it too rushed to take less than one week to canoe from Carswell Lake to the mouth of the William River.

Most difficult is estimating the number of days you will need to canoe along the south shore of Lake Athabasca; wind and waves can make short work of the best-laid plans. William Point to the MacFarlane River is about 100 kilometres, if you follow the curves of all the bays. Always add a few extra days to your travel plans since odds are high that you will encounter rough conditions. We would plan on a minimum of one week to allow sufficient time to explore the dune fields and to account for rough weather. Also work out a back-up plan with your pilot in case you are unable to reach your pick-up point on time.

The best time to visit the dunes is between mid-June and late August. The ice usually doesn't clear from Lake Athabasca until sometime in June and winter can come early. A major advantage of a late summer trip is that mosquito and black fly populations drop off. Early September can also be pleasant, although the weather is more unpredictable.

Saskatchewan communities on Lake Athabasca with scheduled air service include Uranium City, Fond du Lac, and Stony Rapids, the latter having the most frequent service.

A number of communities in northern Saskatchewan have air charter services which visitors can use for canoe trips or other excursions to the Lake Athabasca area. Contact Tourism Saskatchewan (see page 117) for the most current information on operators.

View from the campsite at the small lake in the MacFarlane River.

Athabasca Eco Expeditions

We always used the services of Athabasca Eco Expeditions, based at Otherside River Lodge, about 60 kilometres east of the park and less than 20 kilometres from Fond du Lac. We began and ended many of our trips at the lodge, a welcome place to relax, enjoy home-cooking, and ease our way back into civilization.

Cliff and Stella Blackmur, with close to 25 years' experience, operate Athabasca Eco Expeditions as well as Athabasca Fishing Lodges at Otherside River. They have a close association with Fond du Lac, the home of almost all their guides. Along with providing flights, canoes and other logistics for independent trips throughout the north, they arrange fully guided excursions led by local Dene guides who know the history and culture of the north.

During the summer there are weekly non-stop charter flights between Saskatoon, Saskatchewan and Stony Rapids, where guests are picked up and taken to Otherside River Lodge by float plane or cabin cruiser.

Athabasca Eco Expeditions
P.O. Box 7800
Saskatoon, Saskatchewan, Canada, S7K 4R5
Phone: (306) 653-5490 Fax: (306) 653-5525
1-800-667-5490 (toll-free in North America)
e-mail: athabasca@sk.sympatico.ca
Web site: www.athabascalake.com/ecoexped

The bay at Otherside River Lodge.

Provincial Park Resources

Saskatchewan Environment and Resource Management (SERM), which is responsible for the park, has an information booklet which provides an overview of the sand dunes and explains park regulations. Most of these are common sense rules such as not walking on or disturbing the desert pavement, not disturbing or collecting material such as plants, artifacts and ventifacts, and carrying out all garbage. For the most part, campfires are not allowed in interior areas of the dunes. Where campfires are allowed, such as along the south shore, only dead wood may be used and no wood should be collected from sand dune areas. Camping is not allowed in the dunes west of the William River.

Visitors are asked to check with the SERM office in Stony Rapids or La Ronge before starting a trip. One reason is for safety, so that someone knows where you are and when you are expected to finish your trip. Another reason is to be sure that visitors understand the potential hazards and fragile nature of the area. Contact SERM for a complete list of regulations, as well as updated information. The Stony Rapids office is headed by George Bihun, a long-time area resident who is especially knowledgeable about the sand dunes.

SERM
General Delivery
Stony Rapids, Saskatchewan, Canada, S0J 2R0
Phone: (306) 439-2062 Fax: (306) 439-2036

Cabins at Otherside River Lodge.

For information on the park contact Park Manager Kevin Weatherbee at:

SERM
Box 5000
La Ronge, Saskatchewan, Canada, S0J 1L0
Phone: (306) 425-4288 Fax: (306) 425-2580

You can also contact the SERM Inquiry Centre at (306) 787-2700, or 1-800-667-2757 within Saskatchewan, for more information on provincial parks. SERM's web site is at: www.gov.sk.ca/govt/environ/

Maps

1:50,000 scale topographic maps and aerial photographs are available from:

Saskgeomatics
2151 Scarth Street
Regina, Saskatchewan, Canada, S4P 3V7
Phone: (306) 787-2799 Fax: (306) 787-3335

Topographic maps covering Carswell Lake to William Point:
74 K/11   Tuma Lake
74 K/14   Silverthorne Lake
74 N/3   William Point

Topographic maps covering the south shore of Lake Athabasca from William Point to the falls on the MacFarlane River:
74 N/3   William Point
74 N/2   Cantara Bay
74 N/1   Archibald River
74 0/4   Helmer Lake

Lake Athabasca, 10:30 p.m. on a July evening.

Tourism Saskatchewan

Tourism Saskatchewan can provide updates on visiting Lake Athabasca, as well as information on other ecotours, canoe trips, and the many attractive travel options throughout Saskatchewan.

Major publications available from Tourism Saskatchewan include the annual *Saskatchewan Vacation Guide*, *Fishing and Hunting Guide*, *Events Calendar*, *Saskatchewan Highway Map*, and *Accommodation, Parks and Campground Guide.* Specialty publications covering canoeing, birdwatching, and other activities are also available.

Tourism Saskatchewan
500-1900 Albert Street
Regina, Saskatchewan, Canada, S4P 4L9
Phone: (306) 787-2300 Fax: (306) 787-5744
1-800-667-7191 (toll-free in North America)
e-mail: travel.info@sasktourism.com
Web site: www.sasktourism.com

Appendix I

Check-list of Rare Plants of Saskatchewan's Athabasca Sand Dunes

Endemic felt-leaved willow.

    * Plants considered rare in Saskatchewan
  ** Plants considered rare in Canada
*** Plants endemic to Lake Athabasca's south shore

*** *Achillea lanulosa* ssp. *megacephala*
Large-headed woolly yarrow

  * *Arabis arenicola*
Arctic rock-cress

  * *Arethusa bulbosa*
Dragon's-mouth orchid; Swamp-pink; Arethusa

*** *Armeria maritima* ssp. *interior*
Inland sea-thrift

  * *Calamagrostis lapponica* var. *nearctica*
Lapland reed-grass

  * *Carex cryptolepis*
Yellow sedge

  * *Carex maritima*
Seaside sedge

  * *Carex michauxiana*
Michaux's sedge

  * *Carex pauciflora*
Few-flowered sedge

  * *Carex trisperma*
Three-fruited sedge

  * *Castilleja raupii*
Purple or Northern Paintbrush

  * *Corispermum nitidum*
Neat bug-seed

*** *Deschampsia mackenzieana*
Mackenzie hair-grass

  * *Dichanthelium acuminatum*
Hairy or Woolly panic-grass

 ** *Drosera linearis*
Narrow-leaved sundew

  * *Elymus mollis*
Sea lyme-grass; American dune grass; Dune wild-rye; Strand-wheat

  * *Eriophorum scheuchzeri*
Scheuchzer's cotton-grass

  * *Eriophorum tenellum*
Delicate cotton-grass

* *Euphrasia arctica* var. *disjuncta*
  Eyebright

* *Isoetes macrospora*
  Large-spored quillwort

* *Juncus albescens*
  Pale three-flowered rush

* *Juncus stygius* ssp. *americanus*
  American bog rush; Moor rush

*** *Lechea intermedia* var. *depauperata*
  Impoverished Pinweed

* *Ledum palustre* ssp. *decumbens*
  Narrow-leaved Labrador-tea

* *Luzula multiflora*
  Many-flowered wood-rush

* *Lycopodium inundatum*
  Northern bog club-moss

* *Lycopodium selago* var. *selago*
  Mountain or Northern club-moss or fir-moss

* *Lycopodium selago* var. *appressum*
  Mountain or Northern club-moss or fir-moss

* *Lycopodium sitchense*
  Sitka ground-cedar; Ground-fir

** *Malaxis paludosa*
  Bog adder's-mouth orchid

* *Myriophyllum alterniflorum*
  Alternate-flowered water-milfoil

* *Nymphaea tetragona* ssp. *leibergii*
  Small white water-lily

* *Poa lanata*
  Lanate bluegrass

* *Potamogeton epihydrus*
  Ribbon-leaf pondweed

* *Ranunculus hyperboreus*
  Northern buttercup

* *Rhynchospora fucsa*
  Sooty beaked-rush

* *Sagina nodosa* ssp. *borealis*
  Knotted pearlwort

*** *Salix brachycarpa* var. *psammophila*
  Sand-loving barrenground willow

*** *Salix planifolia* ssp. *tyrrellii*
  Tyrrell's willow

*** *Salix silicicola*
  Felt-leaved willow

*** *Salix turnorii*
  Turnor's willow

* *Scirpus subterminalis*
  Subterminal bulrush

* *Silene acaulis* var. *exscapa*
  Moss-campion

* *Sparganium fluctuans*
  Floating-leaved bur-reed

*** *Stellaria arenicola*
  Sand chickweed

* *Subularia aquatica* ssp. *americana*
  Awlwort

* *Tanacetum huronense* var. *bifarium*
  Indian tansy; Lake Huron tansy

*** *Tanacetum huronense* var. *floccosum*
  Floccose tansy

* *Torreyochloa pallida* var. *fernaldii*
  Pale manna-grass

* *Trientalis europaea* var. *arctica*
  Arctic star-flower

* *Trisetum spicatum*
  Spike trisetum

* *Utricularia cornuta*
  Horned bladderwort

Source: Harms, Vernon L., Peggy Ann Ryan and Judy A. Haraldson. May, 1992. *The Rare and Endangered Native Vascular Plants of Saskatchewan*. Prepared for the Saskatchewan Natural History Society. The W.P. Fraser Herbarium, University of Saskatchewan. Used with permission.

Appendix II

Check-list of Birds—Athabasca Sand Dunes Area

(Compiled in the order of the *Atlas of Saskatchewan Birds* by Alan R. Smith, 1996, updated with the fortieth and forty-first supplements to the American Ornithologists' Union *Check-list of North American Birds*.)

Bald eagle.

Red-throated Loon *(Gavia stellata)*
Pacific Loon *(Gavia pacifica)*
Common Loon *(Gavia immer)*
Yellow-billed Loon *(Gavia adamsii)*
Pied-billed Grebe *(Podilymbus podiceps)*
Horned Grebe *(Podiceps auritus)*
Red-necked Grebe *(Podiceps grisegena)*
American Bittern *(Botaurus lentiginosus)*
Great Blue Heron *(Ardea herodias)*
Tundra Swan *(Cygnus columbianus)*
Trumpeter Swan *(Cygnus buccinator)*
Greater White-fronted Goose *(Anser albifrons)*
Snow Goose *(Chen caerulescens)*
Canada Goose *(Branta canadensis)*
Gadwall *(Anas strepera)*
American Wigeon *(Anas americana)*
American Black Duck *(Anas rubripes)*
Mallard *(Anas platyrhynchos)*
Blue-winged Teal *(Anas discors)*
Northern Shoveler *(Anas clypeata)*
Northern Pintail *(Anas acuta)*
Green-winged Teal *(Anas crecca)*
Ring-necked Duck *(Aythya collaris)*
Lesser Scaup *(Aythya affinis)*
Surf Scoter *(Melanitta perspicillata)*
White-winged Scoter *(Melanitta fusca)*
Oldsquaw *(Clangula hyemalis)*
Bufflehead *(Bucephala albeola)*
Common Goldeneye *(Bucephala clangula)*
Hooded Merganser *(Lophodytes cucullatus)*
Common Merganser *(Mergus merganser)*
Red-breasted Merganser *(Mergus serrator)*
Osprey *(Pandion haliaetus)*
Bald Eagle *(Haliaeetus leucocephalus)*
Northern Harrier *(Circus cyaneus)*
Sharp-shinned Hawk *(Accipiter striatus)*
Northern Goshawk *(Accipiter gentilis)*
Red-tailed Hawk *(Buteo jamaicensis)*
Rough-legged Hawk *(Buteo lagopus)*
Golden Eagle *(Aquila chrysaetos)*

American Kestrel *(Falco sparverius)*
Merlin *(Falco columbarius)*
Spruce Grouse *(Dendragapus canadensis)*
Willow Ptarmigan *(Lagopus lagopus)*
Sharp-tailed Grouse *(Tympanuchus phasianellus)*
Sora *(Porzana carolina)*
American Coot *(Fulica americana)*
Sandhill Crane *(Grus canadensis)*
Semipalmated Plover *(Charadrius semipalmatus)*
Piping Plover *(Charadrius melodus)*
Killdeer *(Charadrius vociferus)*
American Avocet *(Recurvirostra americana)*
Greater Yellowlegs *(Tringa melanoleuca)*
Lesser Yellowlegs *(Tringa flavipes)*
Spotted Sandpiper *(Actitis macularia)*
Hudsonian Godwit *(Limosa haemastica)*
Ruddy Turnstone *(Arenaria interpres)*
Red Knot *(Calidris canutus)*
Sanderling *(Calidris alba)*
Semipalmated Sandpiper *(Calidris pusilla)*
Least Sandpiper *(Calidris minutilla)*
Baird's Sandpiper *(Calidris bairdii)*
Pectoral Sandpiper *(Calidris melanotos)*
Dunlin *(Calidris alpina)*
Stilt Sandpiper *(Calidris himantopus)*
Short-billed Dowitcher *(Limnodromus griseus)*
Long-billed Dowitcher *(Limnodromus scolopaceus)*
Common Snipe *(Gallinago gallinago)*
Wilson's Phalarope *(Phalaropus tricolor)*
Red-necked Phalarope *(Phalaropus lobatus)*
Parasitic Jaeger *(Stercorarius parasiticus)*
Long-tailed Jaeger *(Stercorarius longicaudus)*
Little Gull *(Larus minutus)*
Bonaparte's Gull *(Larus philadelphia)*
Mew Gull *(Larus canus)*
Ring-billed Gull *(Larus delawarensis)*
California Gull *(Larus californicus)*
Herring Gull *(Larus argentatus)*
Glaucous Gull *(Larus hyperboreus)*
Caspian Tern *(Sterna caspia)*
Common Tern *(Sterna hirundo)*
Arctic Tern *(Sterna paradisaea)*

Great Horned Owl *(Bubo virginianus)*
Northern Hawk Owl *(Surnia ulula)*
Great Gray Owl *(Strix nebulosa)*
Common Nighthawk *(Chordeiles minor)*
Belted Kingfisher *(Ceryle alcyon)*
Yellow-bellied Sapsucker *(Sphyrapicus varius)*
Hairy Woodpecker *(Picoides villosus)*
Three-toed Woodpecker *(Picoides tridactylus)*
Black-backed Woodpecker *(Picoides arcticus)*
Northern Flicker *(Colaptes auratus)*
Olive-sided Flycatcher *(Contopus borealis)*
Western Wood-Pewee *(Contopus sordidulus)*
Yellow-bellied Flycatcher *(Empidonax flaviventris)*
Alder Flycatcher *(Empidonax alnorum)*
Eastern Kingbird *(Tyrannus tyrannus)*
Northern Shrike *(Lanius excubitor)*
Blue-headed Vireo *(Vireo solitarius)*
Red-eyed Vireo *(Vireo olivaceus)*
Gray Jay *(Perisoreus canadensis)*
Blue Jay *(Cyanocitta cristata)*
American Crow *(Corvus brachyrhynchos)*
Common Raven *(Corvus corax)*
Horned Lark *(Eremophila alpestris)*
Tree Swallow *(Tachycineta bicolor)*
Bank Swallow *(Riparia riparia)*
Barn Swallow *(Hirundo rustica)*
Black-capped Chickadee *(Parus atricapillus)*
Boreal Chickadee *(Parus hudsonicus)*
Red-breasted Nuthatch *(Sitta canadensis)*
Ruby-crowned Kinglet *(Regulus calendula)*
Gray-cheeked Thrush *(Catharus minimus)*
Swainson's Thrush *(Catharus ustulatus)*
Hermit Thrush *(Catharus guttatus)*
American Robin *(Turdus migratorius)*
European Starling *(Sturnus vulgaris)*
Bohemian Waxwing *(Bombycilla garrulus)*
Cedar Waxwing *(Bombycilla cedrorum)*
Tennessee Warbler *(Vermivora peregrina)*
Orange-crowned Warbler *(Vermivora celata)*
Yellow Warbler *(Dendroica petechia)*
Cape May Warbler *(Dendroica tigrina)*
Yellow-rumped Warbler *(Dendroica coronata)*

Palm Warbler *(Dendroica palmarum)*
Blackpoll Warbler *(Dendroica striata)*
Common Yellowthroat *(Geothlypis trichas)*
Wilson's Warbler *(Wilsonia pusilla)*
Western Tanager *(Piranga ludoviciana)*
Chipping Sparrow *(Spizella passerina)*
Clay-colored Sparrow *(Spizella pallida)*
Vesper Sparrow *(Pooecetes gramineus)*
Savannah Sparrow *(Passerculus sandwichensis)*
Le Conte's Sparrow *(Ammodramus leconteii)*
Fox Sparrow *(Passerella iliaca)*
Song Sparrow *(Melospiza melodia)*
Lincoln's Sparrow *(Melospiza lincolnii)*
Swamp Sparrow *(Melospiza georgiana)*

White-throated Sparrow *(Zonotrichia albicollis)*
White-crowned Sparrow *(Zonotrichia leucophrys)*
Dark-eyed Junco *(Junco hyemalis)*
Lapland Longspur *(Calcarius lapponicus)*
Snow Bunting *(Plectrophenax nivalis)*
Red-winged Blackbird *(Agelaius phoeniceus)*
Rusty Blackbird *(Euphagus carolinus)*
Common Grackle *(Quiscalus quiscula)*
Red Crossbill *(Loxia curvirostra)*
White-winged Crossbill *(Loxia leucoptera)*
Common Redpoll *(Carduelis flammea)*
Pine Siskin *(Carduelis pinus)*
American Goldfinch *(Carduelis tristis)*

Sources:

Abouguendia, Z.M. (ed.) 1981. *Athabasca Sand Dunes in Saskatchewan*. Mackenzie River Basin Study Report, Supplement 7.

Nero, Robert W. 1963. *Birds of the Lake Athabasca Region, Saskatchewan*. Saskatchewan Natural History Society.

Phillips, D. 1991. Saskatchewan Environment and Resource Management. Unpublished field notes.

Roy, J.F. July, 1990. Unpublished field notes.

Smith, Alan R. 1996. *Atlas of Saskatchewan Birds*. Saskatchewan Natural History Society.

APPENDIX III

CHECK-LIST OF MAMMALS—ATHABASCA SAND DUNES AREA

Masked shrew *(Sorex cinereus)*
Northern water shrew *(Sorex palustris)*
Arctic shrew *(Sorex arcticus)*
Pigmy shrew *(Microsorex hoyi)*
Little brown bat *(Myotis lucifugus)*
Big brown bat *(Eptesicus fuscus)*
Hoary bat *(Lasiurus cinereus)*
Snowshoe hare *(Lepus americanus)*
Least chipmunk *(Eutamias minimus)*
Woodchuck *(Marmota monax)*
Red squirrel *(Tamiasciurus hudsonicus)*
Northern flying squirrel *(Glaucomys sabrinus)*
Beaver *(Castor canadensis)*
Deer Mouse *(Peromyscus maniculatus)*
Northern red-backed vole *(Clethrionomys rutilus)*
Gapper's red-backed vole *(Clethrionomys gapperi)*
Northern bog lemming *(Synaptomys borealis)*
Heather vole *(Phenacomys intermedius)*
Muskrat *(Ondatra zibethicus)*
Meadow vole *(Microtus pennsylvanicus)*
Meadow jumping mouse *(Zapus hudsonius)*
Porcupine *(Erethizon dorsatum)*

Coyote *(Canis latrans)*
Wolf *(Canis lupus)*
Arctic fox *(Alopex lagopus)*
Red fox *(Vulpes vulpes)*
Black bear *(Ursus americanus)*
Marten *(Martes americana)*
Fisher *(Martes pennanti)*
Ermine *(Mustela erminea)*
Long-tailed weasel *(Mustela frenata)*
Least weasel *(Mustela nivalis)*
Mink *(Mustela vison)*
Wolverine *(Gulo gulo)*
Striped skunk *(Mephitis mephitis)*
River otter *(Lontra canadensis)*
Lynx *(Lynx lynx)*
Woodland caribou *(Rangifer tarandus caribou)*
Barren-ground caribou *(Rangifer tarandus groenlandicus)*
Mule deer *(Odocoileus hemionus)*
White-tailed deer *(Odocoileus virginianus)*
Moose *(Alces alces)*

Sources:

Abouguendia, Z.M. (ed.). 1981. *Athabasca Sand Dunes in Saskatchewan.* Mackenzie River Basin Study Report, Supplement 7.

Updated by Saskatchewan Environment and Resource Management.

BIBLIOGRAPHY

Abouguendia, Z.M. and W.W. Sawchyn. 1980. *The Athabasca Sand Dunes of Saskatchewan—A Multidisciplinary Study.* Saskatchewan Research Council Publication No. C-805-0-4-E-80.

Abouguendia, Z.M. (ed.). 1981. *Athabasca Sand Dunes in Saskatchewan.* Mackenzie Basin River Study Report, Supplement 7.

Adam, C.I.G. 1987. *Athabasca Sand Dunes Park Land Reserve.* Saskatchewan Parks, Recreation and Culture. Report 87-4.

Banfield, A.W.F. 1974. *The Mammals of Canada.* University of Toronto Press.

Beck, Harvey. 1964. Records of Mammals in the Lake Athabasca Area, Saskatchewan. *The Blue Jay* 22(4):165-172.

Burnett, J.A., C.T. Dauphiné Jr., S.H. McCrindle and T. Mosquin. 1989. *On the Brink, Endangered Species in Canada.* Western Producer Prairie Books, Saskatoon.

David, P.P. 1977. *Sand Dune Occurrences in Canada: A theme and resources inventory study of eolian landforms in Canada.* Parks Canada, Department of Indian and Northern Affairs, Contract No 74-230.

David, P.P. 1981. Stabilized dune ridges in northern Saskatchewan. *Canadian Journal of Earth Sciences* 18:286-310.

Harms, Vernon. L, Peggy Ann Ryan and Judy A. Haraldson. 1992. *The Rare and Endangered Vascular Plants of Saskatchewan.* Prepared for the Saskatchewan Natural History Society. The W.P. Fraser Herbarium, University of Saskatchewan, Saskatoon.

Harms, Vernon L. 1996. COSEWIC Status Report on Impoverished Pinweed (*Lechea intermedia* var. *depauperata*) in Canada. Committee on the Status of Endangered Wildlife in Canada.

Hermesh, R. 1972. *A Study of the Ecology of the Athabasca Sand Dunes with Emphasis on the Phytogenic Aspects of Dune Formation.* M.Sc. thesis, Department of Plant Ecology, University of Saskatchewan, Saskatoon.

Jonker, Peter (ed.). 1992. *Saskatchewan's Endangered Spaces: An Introduction.* Extension Division, University of Saskatchewan, Saskatoon.

Karpan, Robin and Arlene Karpan. 1991. Northern Dunes: The strange ice-age desert of Lake Athabasca, *Canadian Geographic* III (3):42-50.

Karpan, Robin and Arlene Karpan. 1992. Athabasca's Shifting Dunes. *Explore* 55:20-23.

Karpan, Robin and Arlene Karpan. 1995. Dunes. *Western People* 788:3-5.

Karpan, Robin and Arlene, and Parks Facilities Branch, La Ronge Region. 1997. *Athabasca Sand Dunes Provincial Wilderness Park.* Saskatchewan Environment and Resource Management.

Macdonald, S.E., C.C. Chinnappa, D.M. Reid, and B.G. Purdy. 1987. Population differentiation of the *Stellaria longipes* complex within Saskatchewan's Athabasca sand dunes. *Canadian Journal of Botany* 56: 1726-1732.

Macdonald, S.E. and M.D. Macdonald. 1991. Life in a Northern Desert. *Borealis* 2(4): 14-17.

MacLean, P.A. 1984. *Large-scale eolian dunes of the William River area, northern Saskatchewan.* M.Sc. thesis, McGill University, Montreal.

McIntyre. Bernard G. 1993. *Uranium City: The Last Boom Town.* Driftwood Publishers, Mill Bay.

Meyer, David. 1981. Heritage Resources. In Stony Rapids Community and Resource Access Road, Stage II: Environmental Evaluation of Alternative Corridors. MacLaren Plansearch, Saskatoon.

Nero, R.W. 1963. *Birds of the Lake Athabasca Region, Saskatchewan.* Saskatchewan Natural History Society, Regina.

Nero, R.W. 1988. The Ventifacts of the Athabasca Sand Dunes. *Musk-Ox* 36:44-50.

Parker, James. 1987. *Emporium of the North. Fort Chipewyan and the Fur Trade to 1835.* Alberta Culture and Multiculturalism/Canadian Plains Research Center, Regina.

Purdy, B.G. and S.E. Macdonald. 1991. Status Report on the Sand Stitchwort *Stellaria Arenicola* Raup. Committee on the Status of Endangered Wildlife in Canada (COSEWIC).

Purdy, B.G. *Genetic Variation in Endemic Plants of the Athabasca Sand Dunes: Origin, Evolution and Implications for Conservation.* Report prepared for the Endangered Species Recovery Fund, World Wildlife Fund, Canada and the Saskatchewan Department of Parks and Renewable Resources.

Raup, H.M. and G.W. Argus. 1982. *The Lake Athabasca Sand Dunes of northern Saskatchewan and Alberta, Canada. I. Land and vegetation.* National Museum of Natural Sciences, Ottawa.

Rowe, J.S. and Z.M. Abouguendia. 1982. The Lake Athabasca sand dunes of Saskatchewan, a unique area. *Musk-Ox* 30: 1-22.

Rowe, J.S. and R. Hermesh. 1974. Saskatchewan's Athabasca Sand Dunes. *Nature Canada* 3:19-23

Smith, Alan R. 1996. *Atlas of Saskatchewan Birds.* Spec. Publ. No. 22, Saskatchewan Natural History Society, Regina.

Smith, D.G. 1978. *The Athabasca Sand Dunes, A Physical Inventory.* Indian and Northern Affairs, National Parks Branch. Contract No. 77-31.

Smith, D.G. 1980. Saskatchewan's sand dunes, a touch of Araby. *Canadian Geographical Journal* 100 (5):24-29

Tyrrell, J.B. 1896. *Report on the country between Athabasca Lake and Churchill River.* Geological Survey of Canada Annual Report for 1894.

Tyrrell, J.B. (ed.). 1934. *The Journals of Samuel Hearne and Philip Turnor Between the years 1774 and 1792.* Champlain Society, Toronto.

Wright, J.V. 1975. *The Prehistory of Lake Athabasca: An Initial Statement.* National Museum of Man, Mercury Series. Archaeological Survey of Canada, Paper No. 29. National Museums of Canada, Ottawa.

Index

Alberta 15, 16, 31, 33, 37, 98
archaeology 72–73
Archibald River 81, 83, 85–92, 95, 115
Arctic 31, 35, 55, 71–72, 74
Athabasca Eco Expeditions 113
Athabasca Fishing Lodges 113
Athabasca Plain Ecoregion 15
Athabasca River 73–74, 98
beach ridges 6, 47, 55, 57–58, 70–71, 75, 81, 84, 88–89, 91, 95, 101, 107–109
Beaver Point 55–56, 75–80
Beaver River 74, 97
bibliography 124–125
bird check-list 120
birds
    Arctic tern 43, 71, 98, 100
    bald eagle 71, 99, 102
    common loon 71
    killdeer 70
    least sandpiper 71
    piping plover 83
    red-necked phalarope 71
    red-throated loon 71
    sandhill crane 87
    scoters 71
    semipalmated plover 71
    spotted sandpiper 70
    spruce grouse 84, 98–99
bison 73
bear 26, 28, 49, 68–69, 84, 100
Black River 97
blowouts 57–58, 87, 89, 97
Brudell Lake 111
Camsell Portage 74
Cantara Bay 75, 79–81, 115
Cantara Lake 75, 79
caribou 68–70, 72–73
Carswell Lake 16, 18, 70, 89, 111–112, 115
Carswell River 17, 111
Chipewyan 72–73, 97
Churchill River 74, 97
Clearwater River 74
COSEWIC 35
Crackingstone Peninsula 75

Cree Lake 15
Davy Lake 70
Dene 11, 70, 72, 113
desert pavement 37–38, 40–41, 43, 78, 86, 91, 114
Dowling, D.B. 74
Dreikanter 38
dune groups
    dry-sand (desert) dunes 40
    moist-sand (parabolic) dunes 40
dune slacks 36–37
dune styles or types
    longitudinal 45
    oblique sand ridges 45
    parabolic 40, 45
    rolling 41
    seif 45
    transverse 41, 45
East Archibald Lake 81
Einkanter 38
Eldorado Nuclear 78
endemic plants 30–36
exhumed forest 63, 65, 86, 91, 105
Fidler, Peter 73, 97
Fond du Lac 71, 74, 98, 103, 112–113
Fort Chipewyan 74
Fort McMurray 98
Fort Smith 79
fur trade 73–74
Geological Survey of Canada 74, 97
Giant Beaver River 97
Glacial Lake Athabasca 15
glacier 15, 31, 38
Gobi Desert 37
Goldfields 75
Grand Rapid River 97
Great Beaver River 97
Gunnar mine 75
Hale Lake 111
Hudson's Bay Company 73–74, 80, 97
Hudson Bay 35, 74
Ile-à-la-Crosse 97
Inuit 72
Keewatin ice field 15
Lake Athabasca, north shore 72, 74–75, 91

La Loche 74
MacFarlane River 15, 70, 74, 80, 95–98, 102–104, 107, 111–113, 115
mammal check-list 123
Manitoba 98, 106
maps 8, 10, 54, 80, 115
Methye Portage 74
moose 49, 51, 68, 84, 86, 100
Northern Plains culture 73
Northwest Company 73–74
Northwest Territories 70, 79, 98
Otherside River Lodge 70, 113–115
Pacific Ocean 73
photography 105–110
Pond, Peter 73
Precambrian Shield 15
provincial wilderness park 11, 30, 33, 35, 78
rare plant check-list 118
reclamation 36
Reindeer Lake 74
Royal Lake 75
Saskatchewan 15–16, 30, 33, 35, 70, 72, 74, 78, 98, 100, 112, 115, 117
Saskatchewan Environment and Resource Management (SERM) 111, 114–115
Saskatchewan River 74
Saskatoon 36, 113
Saskgeomatics 115
Snare River 111
Stony Rapids 111–114
Thompson, David 74
Thomson Bay 55–58, 62, 65, 68, 74, 79–80, 112
Thomson Bay dune field 24, 26, 29, 55, 79
Tourism Saskatchewan 112, 117
tracks 43, 46, 68–70, 84, 87, 100
Turnor, Philip 73–74, 80, 97
Turnor Point 80, 91
Tyrrell, Joseph Burr 74, 97
uranium 36, 75, 78
Uranium City 71–72, 75, 78, 90, 112
ventifacts 38–40
Vikings 35
Visiting the Athabasca Sand Dunes 111–117
wildlife 68, 70, 100, 102, 110
William Point 55, 70, 115
William River 7, 10–11, 14–15, 17–19, 23–26, 28–31, 35–37, 41, 45–51, 55, 71, 74, 79, 86–87, 89, 96, 105–106, 110–112, 114
William River creek 47–51
William River delta 47–49, 51, 57
William River dune field 15, 18–19, 40, 47
Wilson Creek 81
Wollaston Lake 15, 74
Wolverine Point 91, 95
World War II 75
Yakow dunes 96
Yakow Lake 95, 97, 101

Ordering Information

For additional copies of *Northern Sandscapes* contact your favorite book store. You may also order directly from:

Parkland Publishing
501 Mount Allison Place
Saskatoon, Saskatchewan
Canada S7H 4A9

Phone: (306) 242-7731
Fax: (306) 242-7731
e-mail: parkland@skyport.com
web site: www.skyport.com/parkland/books

Prices subject to change without notice.

In Canada, send a cheque or money order for $36.00 ($29.95 plus $2.10 GST plus $3.95 shipping and handling).

In the United States, send a cheque or money order for $27.95 US currency ($23.95 plus $4.00 shipping and handling).

Outside Canada or the United States, send a money order in US currency for $36.75 ($23.95 plus $12.80 shipping) for delivery by air, or $30.45 ($23.95 plus $6.50 shipping) for delivery by surface.

Contact Parkland Publishing for special pricing and shipping rates on multiple copies.

About the Authors

Robin and Arlene Karpan are writers and photographers based in Saskatoon, Saskatchewan, who have a special interest in the natural environment. Their work has appeared in more than 90 publications around the world, including *Nature Canada*, *Condé Nast Traveler*, *Canadian Geographic*, *GEO*, *Miami Herald*, *Boston Globe* and *Dallas Morning News*. While they travel extensively to many parts of the world, they have found that some of the most exciting natural destinations are close to home in Saskatchewan.

The Karpans also give lectures and slide show presentations on the Athabasca Sand Dunes and other natural areas.

OTHER SERVICES OFFERED BY PARKLAND PUBLISHING

International Stock Photography by Robin and Arlene Karpan. A photographic library of over 40,000 images from around the world including North America, Central America, South America, Caribbean, South Pacific, Asia, and Europe. Images are available for use in publications, brochures, advertisements, and web sites.

Web site:
www.skyport.com/parkland/internat

Saskatchewan Stock Photography by Robin and Arlene Karpan. An extensive photographic library dedicated exclusively to images of Saskatchewan.

Web site:
www.skyport.com/parkland/skphotos/index